T0209846

YOU ARE GOD'S MASTERPIECE,

CREATED IN HIS IMAGE,

ENDOWED WITH HIS ATTRIBUTES,

AND DESIGNED TO SUCCEED IN HIS

WORLD BY USING THE ABILITIES

HE GAVE YOU TO GLORIFY HIM!

Based on Ephesians 2:10

Why You?

You Are God's Masterpiece, Designed to Succeed in His World!

RON EZINGA

WESTBOW
PRESS®
A DIVISION OF THOMAS NELSON
& ZONDERVAN

WestBow Press books may be ordered through booksellers or by contacting:

WestBow Press
A Division of Thomas Nelson & Zondervan
1663 Liberty Drive
Bloomington, IN 47403
www.westbowpress.com
1 (866) 928-1240

ISBN: 978-1-9736-5071-3 (sc)
ISBN: 978-1-9736-5070-6 (hc)
ISBN: 978-1-9736-5072-0 (e)

Library of Congress Control Number: 2019900341

Print information available on the last page.

WestBow Press rev. date: 05/21/2019

CONTENTS

ACKNOWLEDGEMENTS

It would be impossible for me to remember everyone who offered encouragement along the winding road to this book becoming a reality after 15 years. As a first-time author, I often experienced what is called "writer's block." That's when the mind runs dry and you just have to quit until inspired to begin again. Often, that inspiration was triggered by encouragement from family and friends at just the right time. So, a big thank you to all of you, especially to nephew Jeff, brothers-in-law Mart and Ben, and friends Norm, Phyl and Andy for your helpful input along the way.

Since my children and their families were the primary inspiration for this book, I'm dedicating it to them. Thank you, Lord, for my great kids—Karen, Kim, Dave and Kristy—who, along with their spouses and a baker's dozen "grandies," are all your masterpieces! Special thanks to Kristy for all of your time and expertise as a freelance editor. In the face of your siblings' fear of family implosion, you boldly took on the challenge of editing your father's book. (You obviously inherited more than a few genes from the "mad red penner" as I was known during my career.) And extra special thanks to my kids' mom, a remarkable lady named Anne, who in God's providence answered "yes" to a question I asked her over six decades ago. Words can't adequately express my love for you as my wife, best friend and cheerleader. Without your inspiration and gentle encouragement, *Why You?* would not have been written!

PREFACE

Red flags quickly fly in religious circles when words like *money* and *success* are mentioned. That concern is legitimate due to some in those religious circles who have abused their position and, for personal gain, have gone far beyond what the Bible teaches. With that said, however, the Bible does have much to say on every area of life—especially about *money* and *success*.

In fact, Jesus talked more about money than any other aspect of daily living. In Luke 12:16-21, he tells the story about the rich farmer who decides to build bigger barns to store his abundance so he could live the rest of his life in luxury. It's important to see that he didn't condemn the farmer for his riches, but for his greed. In verse 21, Jesus provides a simple warning for those who live solely to achieve material success: "A person is a fool to store up earthly wealth but not have a rich relationship with God."

In addition to Jesus' frequent references to money, the book of Proverbs is jam-packed with teachings on money and profit. And books like Deuteronomy, Ecclesiastes and many in the New Testament offer insights into God's view of how his people should handle their material blessings. It is obvious from those references that obedience is the key to a relationship with him and his blessing.

If all of that is true, it's fair to ask that oft-asked question: *Why do bad things happen to good people?* It may be fair to ask, but that question is impossible for any human to answer. Theologians can only speculate about why missionaries are murdered on the mission field; or a head-on car crash wipes out a family; or cancer takes the life of an innocent child. No one can comprehend the mind of God when these tragedies strike. Only he knows the answer to those questions.

However, it is clear that there are cause-and-effect biblical principles that can be generally applied to our human existence. Simply put, doing good usually has good results and doing bad has bad results. While there is much about life in a chaotic world that we can't understand, of one thing we can be absolutely sure: somehow, God is working out his eternal plan, and in that plan he has a purpose for each life.

We can be thankful if we are living in a society whose laws encourage free enterprise and incorporate godly principles of right and wrong. In that context, people usually prosper because individual effort and investment are rewarded. But with those blessings comes God's warning in Deuteronomy 8:11: "Beware that in your plenty, you do not forget the Lord your God and disobey his commands."

It is my hope that this book will help you find the purpose and balance in your life that enables you to enjoy God's good gifts while sharing them with others to his honor and glory. And when your life ends, I pray that God will welcome you into heaven with Jesus' words from Matthew 25:21, "Well done, my good and faithful servant."

Saved by His Amazing Grace,
Ron Ezinga

INTRODUCTION

Do you think God wants YOU to succeed?

Everyone desires an authentic and successful life that has purpose, but that can only be achieved by following the rules of the game. Though life is not a "game" as we normally think of them, one crucial commonality between life and games is the need for rules. A game without rules can't even be played. Rules give a game meaning. Without them, those trying to play it will quickly get frustrated and give up.

Life is no different. There are rules and guidelines that need to be followed. Without them, people will get frustrated, give up, and look for satisfaction in all the wrong places. Those guidelines for life are all found in the Bible - a book that more people have purchased than any other book ever written. It has sold more copies than all the health, relationship and financial "how-to" books combined. It is the greatest "how-to" book of all times, having changed more lives than any other. It is literally God's handbook for success in every dimension of human life!

Think about it this way: when you buy a new appliance, you get an owner's operating manual with guidelines for its use. By following those guidelines, you will get the most benefit from it. Ignore them and you will have problems. The Bible is God's "Operating Manual." It provides common-sense guidelines for getting the most out of life. Ignoring those guidelines will create problems or issues for us.

So, if a meaningful, successful life is your desire, and you know there's room for improvement in your life—and you're ready to work on making those improvements—keep reading. If you're not ready to do that, keep reading anyway!

Why You? isn't "just another" religious book, though it is based on biblical principles. Regardless of what you've been told or think, the

Bible is not an out-of-date, stodgy old book filled with dos and don'ts. Sure, it has those, but it offers so much more. It's loaded with common sense for life. These words from Proverbs 2:7 make that very clear: "God grants a treasure of common sense to the honest."

Why You? offers insights and guidance based on that "treasure of common sense"—something none too common in today's world. You will learn how to achieve that desired meaningful life, and how to deal with life's difficult questions and issues which we all face. The abundance of "how-to" content found in the Bible can be best described by this simple acronym:

Breakthrough **I**nformation **B**ringing **L**ifelong **E**ncouragement

To illustrate this, King Solomon—who received great wisdom from God—said this in Ecclesiastes 2:24: "There is nothing better than to enjoy food and drink and to find satisfaction in work . . . these pleasures are from the hand of God." That's *Lifelong Encouragement!*

The apostle Paul, who was about as anti-Christian as anyone could be—until he was struck by lightning and went blind while persecuting Christians—said this about people in 1 Timothy 6:17: "Their trust should be in God, who richly gives us all we need for our enjoyment." That's *Lifelong Encouragement!*

Even more incredible and amazing are the words found in John 10:10 spoken by Jesus himself: "My purpose is to give them a rich and satisfying life." That's *Lifelong Encouragement!*

In fact, what Proverbs 1:3 says about the proverbs themselves can be applied to the whole Bible: "Their purpose is to teach people to live disciplined and successful lives, and to help them do what is right, just and fair." That's *Lifelong Encouragement!*

There is nothing stodgy about those encouraging statements—and many more like them—which are found in the Bible. And they certainly don't sound like either failure or simply surviving was God's plan for us, do they? The evidence is overwhelming that:

God <u>does</u> want YOU to succeed in his world!

_____**SPOILER ALERT:**

Whether or not you consider yourself to be a "religious" person, this book will help you identify the key ingredients of true success, many of which you already have. And it will guide you in putting them into practice in *your* life! So, you can't afford to miss chapter 3 entitled "God's Attributes are *Your* Attributes." God created you in his image, and in doing that, he planted his *attributes* in you. Developing those attributes into *life skills* will help you be more successful in using the unique *abilities* God gave you. An understanding of that simple concept will change your life—don't miss it!

WHY YOU? WHY HERE? WHY NOW? NOW WHAT?

If you're like most of us, you have probably had questions at times like: Who am I? Why do I exist here and now? What is the meaning of my life? Is there a purpose for my existence? Am I the accidental or incidental result of a moment of passion? What makes my life worth living? Is it money, career, toys, sports or other stuff which won't last—just as I won't? Or is life just a random "survival of the fittest" until I'm no longer fit, then I die and float among the clouds with others who became unfit?

Obviously, there's more to human life than just existing for a few years and then floating off to the "great beyond"—wherever that is! Through his prophet in Jeremiah 29:11 (NIV), God said, "I know the plans I have for you . . . plans to prosper you . . . plans to give you hope and a future." Certainly doesn't sound like he planned for us to just drift aimlessly through life, does it? Yet that's exactly what many people do, even some who have everything money can buy.

It's thought by many that Mark Twain made this interesting observation: "The two most important days in your life are the day you are born and the day you find out why." To "find out why" you need to answer questions like those posed in the opening paragraph. Those answers will help you discover who you are and why you exist—your purpose in life. And if you understand your purpose, you will be a happier person. So where do you find those answers?

A GOOD PLACE TO START: AT THE BEGINNING

Let's start by looking at how we came to exist in human form on planet earth. There are two predominant theories on this. One is that we are here by pure chance as the product of an evolutionary process started by the Big Bang. The second theory of our origin as humans is that we are who and where we are by the divine plan of the Almighty God who created the universe and everything in it, including us.

First, consider the teaching of evolution. It all started with a small amount of matter and some sort of huge, galactic explosion called the Big Bang. They say this occurred over 13 billion years ago and lasted less than ten seconds, during which the entire universe came into being. And it has been evolving ever since. One skeptic said the chances of that happening are about as good as throwing 26 letters into the air and having Webster's dictionary land at your feet!

The Big Bang theorists believe that as animals evolved over billions of years, at some point, a monkey that was almost human gave birth to a fully human baby. Doubters have called this process "the goo to the zoo to you" theory! As silly as that sounds, it's not too far off from the creation story which tells us that God made Adam from dust—the main ingredient in goo with a little water added! The theory of evolution places us randomly in a universe that just happened all those years ago, with no reason for being, no purpose in living, and no eternal destiny. There is no evolution textbook because there are vast differences in science about exactly when and how the Big Bang happened, and how all that followed it transpired.

Now consider the theory of creation. It teaches that you are who you are and where you are through the plan of a loving, almighty God who created the universe and everything in it, including you. The Bible is the textbook for the theory of divine creation. The book of Genesis goes into great detail about how the universe and all that is in it were created by Almighty God. Chapter 1:31 says: "Then God looked over all he had made, and he saw that it was very good!"

It should be noted that many Christians believe in theistic evolution, which allows for the days detailed in the creation story to be much longer than 24 hours. But all who believe in divine creation would agree that God certainly had the power to complete creation in 24 hour days—or even in 24 seconds! In fact, Hebrews 11:3 puts it this way:

"The entire universe was formed at God's command." Could it be that the Big Bang of evolution was actually God's creation command?

While there certainly are many unanswered questions relating to divine creation, there are that many—and a lot more—about the theory of evolution. For instance, what was there to cause the Big Bang that began the evolutionary process those billions of years ago? If there was some "matter" there, how did *it* get there? And, if the earth is a round sphere spinning in space, what keeps it there, and why don't the oceans spill over? The obvious answer is gravity, but how did gravity come into existence if not created? Gravity couldn't just happen, and hopefully it isn't evolving!

OUR CREATOR DID NOT EVOLVE!

As opposed to those questions and many like them, if you take God at his word—which is usually a good thing to do—Genesis 2:1 leaves little doubt about the origin of our universe: "So the creation of the heavens and the earth and everything in them was completed." Proof of that creative genius is in and all around us. The marvelous complexity of our human bodies—and of all living creatures—provides indisputable proof of creation. Doesn't it stretch credibility beyond the breaking point to believe that all the vital organs in our bodies needed for life—different for male and female—evolved and started working simultaneously at a precise moment all by chance?

Further evidence of creation is found in a universe crammed full of amazing stuff. Consider the African bombardier beetle. It has dual tanks in its body, one carrying hydrogen peroxide and the other hydroquinone. By themselves, these are harmless fluids, but they make poison if mixed. When in danger, the beetle mixes these fluids internally, and through a rotating nozzle it is equipped with, it can shoot the poisonous mixture all directions to blind its attacker. Surely evidence of divine creation. Shades of *Star Wars* in the beetle world!

Consider the intricacies of a tiny hummingbird which hovers on tireless wings, changes direction in a microsecond, and flies hundreds of miles to escape winter. Or the large arctic tern that flies over 10,000 miles from pole to pole and back again every year, staying in warmer climates both ways. Or the gigantic whales that swim thousands of miles to get their favorite food. Or freshwater fish which absorb water through their skin, while fish living in salt water drink it and eliminate the salt through their gills.

Interesting, too, that fish sleep under water, but with their eyes open—they don't have eyelids to close. Dolphins also sleep, but they need to come up for air because if they didn't, they'd drown. To solve that problem, only half of their brain goes to sleep at a time so the other half can decide when it's time to get up and get some air. This split brain in dolphins has been proved by EEG studies of them. These are just a few examples of thousands of fascinating tidbits in the natural world which point to the miracle of divine creation.

Have you ever been awed by an evening sky set ablaze by the setting sun, or gazed at the millions of sparkling stars on a dark night, or been mesmerized by the sound of mighty ocean waves? Only a creator God could hang the sun in the sky in such a way that we don't burn up; throw the stars into the cosmos and keep them there; and fill the oceans with water that doesn't slosh out as the earth rotates! Romans 1:20 makes this statement: "Ever since the world was created, people have seen the earth and sky. Through everything God made, they can clearly see . . . his eternal power and divine nature." So God's creation gives us a window through which we can get a glimpse of his creative power and his eternal control of our universe. Amazing!

THE WOW FACTOR IN GOD'S STRATEGIC PLAN

There are even touches of humor present in creation. Ever wonder what Adam thought when he first saw an ostrich—a bird with wings that can't fly but can outrun a horse? There may also be a little humor in how Adam and Eve met the very first time. After God created Adam, he placed him in paradise, and gave him the responsibility of caring for it. But that was a lot of work, so God decided he should have a helper.

In Genesis 2, we read that God put Adam into a deep sleep and created Eve from one of his ribs.

When Adam woke up and saw Eve, some translations of the Bible say that he intoned, "bone of my bone." But others translate Adam's reaction as being more of an exclamatory statement. In fact, the New Living Translation translated it as "at last!" In today's jargon, that might be translated as "Wow!" or maybe even "Cool!" No doubt Adam was excited with God's provision for him. Having Eve as his helpmate—and lover—probably put new spring in his step as Adam went about his duties in paradise!

THE BOTTOM LINE:

Seriously, the real "wow" factor is that we have a God who is big enough to create and maintain the massive universe in which the earth is just a tiny dot. Yet he is small enough to care about and have a purpose for all of us, including you! Though we don't always understand the twists and turns the highway of life takes, when we look into life's rearview mirror, we can usually see the connection of past experiences to who, why and where we are today. They all have significance in fulfilling God's plan and purpose for us.

You Were Created To Succeed

The dictionary defines *success* as "accomplishing a purpose." In the previous chapter, we saw that God has a purpose for your life. He even created you in his image! If there's any doubt in your mind about that, look at Genesis 1:27 where it says that "God created human beings in his own image . . . male and female he created them." And Psalm 8—a beautiful "creation psalm"—tells us in verses 5-6 that God created people a little lower than himself, and he put all things under their authority.

There are only two options here, folks. God either created us to succeed or to fail! Singer Ethel Waters, who was the product of her teenage mother's rape, is quoted as saying, "God don't make no junk!" You might question her theological credentials but that statement is spot on. Clearly, God would not create us in his image, a little lower than himself, and make us rulers over creation if he planned for us to fail. No way. God created us to succeed, not to be mediocre or just survive—and certainly not to fail!

A BIG OOPS—THE WRONG TREE!

Genesis 1:31 records God's view of creation before he made Adam and Eve: "God looked over all he had made, and he saw that it was very good." But soon after they arrived on the scene, things weren't so "very good." They chose to eat fruit from the wrong tree when tempted by Satan, and that choice changed human life from then on. Their disobedience brought sin into the world, and all humanity since carries their "sin DNA." Their choice became the prime example of how our choices affect not only ourselves but others as well.

At this point, you may be wondering how Adam and Eve's failure could taint you, because you feel you're a fairly good person. Well, "fairly good" doesn't cut it. Let's dig just a tad deeper. Have you ever lied, or lusted, or gossiped, or had evil thoughts or desires, or been selfish, mean, angry, covetous, critical, proud or any number of other evidences of sin's reach? If you admit to any of these, then you're a lying, lustful, selfish, proud, critical, angry, covetous sinner like the rest of us. But if you answer "no" to all these, congratulations—you are one of only two perfect humans to ever walk the face of this earth—just Jesus and you!

You may be a really good person, but the Bible says this in Romans 3:23: "Everyone has sinned; we all fall short of God's glorious standard." Sad but true, all means all, and that's really bad news. But there's also really good news. Sin didn't change how God sees us or his purpose for our lives. He loved us so much that, like any human father would be willing to give his life for his own child, God gave himself in the person of Jesus to die for those who confess their sinfulness. In that way, we can be reconciled with our Creator—the one, only true God. That's his eternal life insurance plan. It has no fine print, it takes immediate effect, and its premium is paid in full!

God wonderfully created us, and even more wonderfully, restored the dignity of our human nature. He no longer sees us as critical, proud, envious, lying, selfish sinners because he looks at us through Jesus. By faith in him, God gives us a purpose for living. Can there be any doubt that you—yes, you—were created to succeed?

THE BOTTOM LINE:

God not only created us and gave us a purpose for living, he also equipped us with unique abilities to fulfill that purpose. Look at what the apostle Paul said about that purpose in Ephesians 2:10: "We are God's masterpiece. He has created us anew in Jesus, so we can do the good things he planned for us long ago." That's a purpose with promise!

THIRTY MINUTES THAT WILL CHANGE YOUR LIFE!

If you read nothing else in this book, read the next two chapters. But before starting them, read the following statement at least three times:

I AM GOD'S MASTERPIECE,
CREATED IN HIS IMAGE,
ENDOWED WITH HIS
ATTRIBUTES AND DESIGNED
TO SUCCEED IN HIS WORLD
BY USING THE ABILITIES
HE GAVE ME TO GLORIFY
HIM! THANK YOU, GOD!

NOW BUCKLE YOUR SEAT BELT
AND HANG ON . . .

God's Attributes Are Your Attributes

We are God's masterpieces. We were created in his image to succeed in doing good things he planned for us. What were the good things God planned for us to do? We need not get deep in theological weeds to answer that question because it's just common sense. In order for his world to function well, God requires people who are good citizens, faithful marriage partners, loving parents, fair employers, productive employees, and the list can go on.

Simply put, whatever we do on a daily basis for our good, the good of others, and to honor God are the good things he planned for us to do. That may sound like an impossible dream because we often fail to live up to God's expectations. Fortunately, God loves his people not because of who they are, but because of who he is. Having created us in his image, he continues to patiently work in our lives to renew us as his masterpieces.

You may wonder what "created in his image" really means and why it's important. Though that statement seems quite clear, what does it really mean? Do we physically look like God? Are we like him mentally? Or emotionally? Over the centuries, these questions have produced much speculation without definitive answers. Is it possible that one answer could be hiding in plain sight? Though his image may not transfer to us physically, it most certainly includes the qualities of God's character commonly called his *attributes*. It could be said that these attributes transfer to us as spiritual DNA from his image. Or, to think of it another way, God's attributes are planted in us as part of his image, and through proper nurturing, they can mature in us and become the basic ingredients for a successful life.

LIKE A PRODUCTIVE GARDEN

To better understand this concept, visualize a beautiful garden where the plants are healthy and loaded with ripe fruits and vegetables. Now think about what it took to get that garden to the point of a successful harvest. The soil needed to be prepared, seeds had to be planted, water and fertilizer had to be applied. And once the seedlings sprouted, they had to be cultivated and the weeds had to be pulled. Anyone who has had a garden knows the immense amount of effort and cost that goes into it before it produces fruit. Many who have experienced all the hassle and expense that a garden involves are now strong patrons of their local farmers markets!

A truly successful life looks much like a successful garden. Our creator God is the master gardener. Just as seeds are planted in a garden, he "planted" his attributes in us. Like seeds in a garden, those attributes in us need constant attention. We must nourish and cultivate those attributes until they sprout and mature into life skills in our lives. During that process, we must continue to pull the "weeds"—the negative influences and issues—from our lives.

IDENTIFYING THE LIFE SKILLS OF TRUE SUCCESS

Have you ever looked at some folks and wondered what makes them so successful in all areas of life? Their "garden" seems to be free of weeds and is producing what the Bible calls the "fruits of the Spirit." That is what Galatians 5:22-23 refers to where it says: "The Holy Spirit produces this kind of fruit in our lives: joy, peace, patience, kindness, goodness, faithfulness, gentleness, and self-control." These sound like godly attributes, right? And Philippians 4:8 provides an obvious clue as to how we need to cultivate those attributes into a productive life: "Fix your thoughts on what is true, and honorable, and right, and pure, and lovely, and admirable. Think about things that are excellent and worthy of praise." Further, in verse 9 Paul tells us to put what he teaches into "practice." That's crucial!

With that clue in mind, think about someone you feel is truly successful—not just financially, but in all dimensions of life. Now, look at the words below and circle those that describe the qualities that you see in that person. Note the similarity of these words to the fruits of the Spirit listed in the previous paragraph, and to those qualities which Paul said we should think about and practice:

Confident   Considerate   Conscientious   Content   Decisive Dependable   Disciplined   Encouraging   Faithful   Forgiving   Friendly Generous   Honest   Humble   Industrious   Kind   Loyal   Optimistic Patient   Prompt

It's likely that you circled most of these to describe that person you had in mind. He or she has succeeded in turning these godly *attributes* into *life skills*. Most truly successful people will exhibit all these characteristics and more. As you look at the list above, do you see any that would *not* fit on Paul's list of "things that are excellent and worthy of praise," or on the "fruits of the Spirit" list? They would all fit, and more could be added. Now look again at that list of attributes God planted in us as part of his image and consider these questions:

1. Would you object if others used these words to describe you? *Don't think so!*

2. Do you see words on this list that you wouldn't want to be? *Hopefully not!*

3. Do you see any you could improve on in your own life? *Of course—we all do!*

4. Can you turn any of them into your life skills? *Sure you can!*

5. Will it take effort on your part? *Sure it will!*

6. Will it change your life? *Absolutely!*

NO TWO FLAKES—OR PEOPLE—ARE ALIKE

This doesn't imply that people are flakes though that might be an apt description of some! The point is that God didn't create us as clones of one another. In God's creation there are literally no two things exactly alike. Here's an amazing fact you can google to verify: of all the snowflakes that have ever fallen, there have never been two of them exactly alike! Rather obviously then, in all of human history, there have never been two people exactly alike. Except for identical twins, we all have different human DNA. But since we have all been created in God's image, his DNA (think attributes) is the same in all of us!

YOUR ATTRIBUTES CAN BECOME LIFE SKILLS

Actually, the process of turning your *attributes* into *life skills* is not all that complicated. That's not to say it's easy. But most things worth doing aren't easy, right? Here's a very simple example. Let's assume that one of your personal strengths is friendliness. Those who know you would say that you're a friendly person. So friendliness is a life skill you have already developed. Your immediate response to this might be a somewhat sarcastic, "Well, big deal." And you'd be right. It is a big deal—a life-changing big deal!

GROUCHY OR FRIENDLY?

Not convinced of how big a deal that is? Let's suppose you were grouchy instead of friendly. You'll have to agree that grouchiness is *not* a godly attribute. So, God could *not* have created you as a grouch. You became a grouch because of various circumstances, choices and other factors in your life. Just imagine the positive change that would take place in your life if, as a grouch, you practiced the attribute of friendliness until it became a life skill. That would be a life changer! Beware . . . grouches who start practicing being friendly should be ready for some strange looks from those who know them as grouches!

To carry this "grouch" example a bit further, Paul challenged us to do more than just *think* about what is excellent and praiseworthy. He also said to *practice* them. If you are a grouchy person, you can say you want to be friendly, but if all you do is think about it and never practice it, you will continue to be a grouch, right? Don't even try to claim that grouches can't practice being friendly. Of course they can! Would any athlete, pianist, plumber, doctor or teacher become successful without practice? In fact, what many know as student teaching is also called "practice" teaching. To do anything well takes practice. Without practice, no one would succeed at anything!

PRACTICE MAKES PERFECT . . . NOT!

At some point, what you're regularly practicing becomes part of you. You hardly have to think about it to get it right. For instance, professional golfers have practiced so much that their swing is almost automatic. But even pros occasionally hit errant shots, so they keep practicing to avoid losing the skill they've developed. The same principle applies to practicing attributes until they become life skills, then continuing to use them in day-to-day life. Sadly, true perfection is impossible, but practice is the key to developing life skills, too.

Actually, the example of pro golfers illustrates well how, through practice, they have developed a few attributes into life skills. For instance, even if no one is looking, they practice *honesty* when they call penalties on themselves if they accidentally violate a rule. They are *persistent* when they don't quit because they're playing poorly. They are *patient* because they know that impatience will quickly ruin their careers. And they show *respect* when they remove their hats and shake hands with their opponents at the end the round. Beware . . . anyone who takes the game of golf even half seriously knows that if you're working on the life skill of patience or even honesty, a bad shot can quickly set back any progress you've made!

THE BOTTOM LINE:

We are all originals, designed by God himself! Ephesians 2:10 says that we are "God's masterpiece." None of us can claim to be self-made individuals. But as his masterpieces who have his attributes, God made all of us capable of making the right choices and decisions in life. And to make his world functional, God gave people different interests and, more importantly, different abilities. Through continuous practice, truly successful people develop their attributes into life skills that empower them to use those abilities. Your success is measured by what you accomplish using your abilities to serve God and others—not what others accomplish using theirs. Your abilities are God's gift to you. Use them to his glory as your gift back to him!

Ron Ezinga

Unlocking Your Life Skills

The following process unlocks the secret to masterpiece living. It is included here to provide an understanding of the steps involved in life skill development. To keep your book unmarked here, this process is also found on page 116 of Life Skill Resources. There, along with implementation instructions, it also includes Life Skill Development tools designed for life skill practice and monitoring

To summarize what Paul suggests in Philippians 4:8-9, we should think about things that are excellent and worthy of praise—things that are true, honorable, right, pure, lovely and admirable. He said we should practice these things. With that in mind, look again at these life skills and see if any would not qualify as true and honorable:

Confident   Considerate   Conscientious   Content   Decisive Dependable   Disciplined   Encouraging   Faithful   Forgiving   Friendly Generous   Honest   Humble   Industrious   Kind   Loyal   Optimistic Patient   Prompt

Now, after thoughtfully considering each life skill, affirm that:

- All of them would fit on Paul's list of "those things that are excellent and worthy of praise."

- If you really wanted to, you could practice every one of them in your everyday life.

- They all have an opposite word that is a negative life issue. For example: Humble—*Proud*, Patient—*Impatient*.

- Each word on the list exists in you, sometimes or all the time, in either a positive or negative way.

Assuming your agreement with these four statements, it's fair to think you'd also agree that by practicing all 20 listed life skills, they could become your life skills. Committing a few minutes of daily practice to the following simple process for the next few months will dramatically improve the rest of your life. This process will help you easily identify the life skills you have and are doing well with; those you have that need more practice; and some that need a lot of work.

1. Set aside 30 minutes when you can be somewhere quiet to carefully review this life skills list without interruption.

2. Honestly ask yourself this question about every life skill on the list: *Am I normally a* (Humble) *person?*

3. Objectively rate yourself for each on this scale: *1-low, 2-average, 3-high*. Jot that rating and date in the first column behind each life skill on the Life Skill Development Tool.

4. After rating and recording all 20 life skills per #3, complete a Life Skill Practice Form for each one. Sort them by rating.

5. Those you rated *1-low* are your first priority to work on, so keep them with you to review and practice every day.

6. After you see progress in your *1s*, carry with you those you rated *2* (from #4) while continuing to work on the *1s*.

7. On a monthly basis, refer back to your original rating list and repeat steps #2-6, objectively re-rating each life skill.

Reminder: The development tool and practice form referred to in steps 3 and 4 are found in the Life Skill Resources along with a duplicate of this 7-step process. Use it there to keep your book unmarked here.

THE KEY TO YOUR SUCCESS

Ever wonder why we are so blessed to live where opportunity rather than oppression exists? That can only happen in countries where individual freedom is an "umbrella" under which there are many important principles that contribute to the opportunity to succeed in life. These principles make up the cultural foundations of developed countries. Without them, the economies and cultures of nations would collapse. With them, economic and cultural strength will not only survive but thrive!

The same umbrella of principles that influence countries and cultures are key to individual success as well. Guided by those principles within the context of a free enterprise system that rewards individual effort, anyone can be financially successful in life. Of course, that can only happen where opportunity is reasonably available to all who are willing to work hard and who are determined to use their God-given abilities. Although that kind of opportunity is not generally available to people in many developing countries, some do succeed anyway through hard work and ingenuity!

So, what is the source of that umbrella of principles that so dramatically affect cultures and human life? It could rightly be said that freedoms come from a nation's laws, but where do those laws come from? It shouldn't be surprising that most—if not all—cultural principles come right out of the Bible! In the Old Testament of the Bible, God gave us a few practical rules for living that have become the main ingredients in the basic laws of western societies.

ALL FOUR LETTER WORDS AREN'T BAD

By now you may have guessed the word implied by the title of this chapter as "the key to success." It's *obey*—a four-letter word that's okay to say and even better to practice! It wields life-changing power, as Adam and Eve found out the hard way. They were created perfect by God, but they (we all would have done the same!) chose to disobey God, and the issues they faced as a result were many.

Greed, pride, jealousy, hatred, murder and many other issues were all present in the life of the first human family. And those issues quickly polluted their perfect world as they do to this day, corrupting the culture we live in. Not much has changed since that tragic choice made in paradise to disobey, has it? Most, if not all, the issues we face in life are direct or indirect results of disobedience—in other words, not following the instructions in God's "Operating Manual!"

THE POWER ISN'T OURS—THE RESPONSIBILITY IS
Here's what God said about the connection between obedience and success in Deuteronomy 8:6: "Obey the commands of the Lord your God by walking in his ways." Then in verse 18, he warns us: "Remember the Lord your God. He is the one who gives you power to be successful." Could it be any clearer than that? But read it again and you'll see that it *doesn't* say that God gives us success; it *does* say that he gives us "power to be successful." So the power comes from God and is released by our obedience. It is our responsibility to exercise that power.

To understand that concept more clearly, think about the family unit and the relationship between parents and their children. Obeying parental rules releases power into the lives of children. That's no different than in God's family—as his sons and daughters, obeying his rules releases power into our lives. In both cases, disobedience ruptures the relationship and restrains the power.

Obedience wields great power over life's issues and yields great rewards in our lives. It has a great deal to do with our having the right attitudes and making the right choices. And the need to obey doesn't end at a certain age. In fact, we are still like children, needing to be reminded of what to do—and not do—along life's path.

THEY'RE COMMANDMENTS—NOT SUGGESTIONS!

So, you may ask, what's to obey? Well, God did give us a few very practical rules for the game of life in his Operating Manual. They're found in Deuteronomy 5:6-21. You should note that they are called the Ten *Commandments*—*not* the Ten *Suggestions*! The first four deal with our relationship with God, while the last six deal with our human relationships. Let's take a brief look at those last six.

- **Commandment #5: "Honor your father and mother."**
  This is often called the "commandment with promise" because the second part of it spells out the benefit of obeying it: "that you will live a long, full life in the land the Lord your God is giving you." What a promise that is! Can there be any doubt that obeying our parents as children makes it much more likely that we have the power to comply with the last five below? Simple as they look, when you think about their implications for social and individual well-being, they are profoundly important. They are the glue that hold individual lives and any country's culture together.

- **Commandment #6: "You must not murder."**

- **Commandment #7: "You must not commit adultery."**

- **Commandment #8: "You must not steal."**

- **Commandment #9: "You must not testify falsely."**

- **Commandment #10: "You must not covet."**

Pretty straightforward stuff, but so important! It's "politically correct" to say that morality can't be legislated. But PC is dead wrong on this one, because these five commandments form the foundation of moral laws in all western societies. For centuries past and to this day, these five commandments have served as the moral and legal underpinnings of what is right and wrong in cultures far and wide. The moral strength of any nation and its citizens is measured by how well those laws are enforced and obeyed. Can you imagine how much happier this world would be if everyone obeyed these last five commandments, thereby avoiding all the social ills they entail?

_____**THE BOTTOM LINE:**

Here's God's challenge and promise: *obey* his commands and he will give us the *power* to be successful. God created us as responsible human beings and we must obediently live according to his principles. Our obedience is the key to exercising God's power. Then, and only then, can we experience masterpiece living!

THE FOUNDATION FOR YOUR SUCCESS

Have you ever visited any of the world's major cities and looked up at those towering skyscrapers? They are amazing! You have to look down, though, to see the most important part of the building—the foundation. It determines whether the skyscraper will support the structure above and survive nature's strongest storms. Similarly, human lives must be built on a strong foundation to support a productive life and survive life's challenging storms. Jesus spoke about that in Matthew 7:24-27 where he said: "Anyone who listens to my teaching and follows it is wise, like a person who builds a house on solid rock . . . But anyone who hears my teaching and doesn't obey it is foolish, like a person who builds a house on sand."

Building and maintaining the right foundation for a truly successful life is a huge challenge! It takes ongoing effort because our need to live in obedience to God's principles is in constant tension with the natural inclinations and desires of our human nature. Our good intentions and the effort to live good lives can help overcome those human inclinations to do the wrong thing. In reality, however, a truly successful life is only possible if it is built on a solid bedrock foundation of faith in God.

A DEADLY ALTERNATIVE

Anyone seriously questioning this matter of faith must consider the common alternative, which is fate. Life is lived in the context of either having faith in God, or believing in fate. And there's a fine line between the two. For instance, fate determines an inevitable course of events in your life, including your eternal destiny. You have no choice in it and can't change it. Conversely, faith in God says we're here by our creator God's design and everything happens within his control. Faith acts as a rearview mirror by which we can see how God has guided us through life's twists and turns. Faith gives purpose to our lives on earth and gives us the assurance of eternal life when we die.

The importance of faith to life is best illustrated by a puzzle. When you start a puzzle, you have faith that all the pieces are there. If, at the end, one piece is missing, the puzzle is incomplete. Really frustrating, right? Similarly, without faith there's a large, God-shaped piece missing in the puzzle of our lives. Earlier we saw that someone referred to the second most important day in your life as the day you find out why you were born. That was probably a reference to finding that God-shaped piece called faith which gives life purpose. Without that piece, life is incomplete and just a frustrating game of chance!

STAND FOR SOMETHING OR FALL FOR ANYTHING

What we believe is determined by who we believe. In the absence of faith in a God, some people fall for false theories like atheism which says there is no God. If there's no God, who assigns basic human dignity? Who says that anything is right or wrong? If you don't believe in a God, how did you get here? What is your reason for existence? It is impossible for atheism or other non-Christian religions to correctly answer those questions and many more.

What is faith and why does it matter so much? A simple definition of faith comes from the Merriam-Webster dictionary: "Faith is a firm belief in something for which there is no proof." Faith matters because it gives meaning to life and hope for the future. Without it, there's no purpose for living here and no hope for eternal life in the hereafter. That old saying fits here: "If you don't stand for something, you'll fall for anything!"

EVERYONE PRACTICES FAITH EVERY DAY

Some say they don't understand faith. But whether we understand it or not, we all exercise a form of faith in many ways every day. For example, do you understand electricity, or do you just flip on a light switch—by faith? Do you understand the mechanics of a car's ignition system, or do you just turn the key or push a button—by faith? Do you understand how all the weeds, bugs and grain that cows eat turn into nutritious milk, or do you just drink it—by faith?

Life is full of things like electricity, ignition and milk that we don't understand but accept by faith, because the lights go on, the motor starts and we don't die from drinking milk, right? Faith could be defined as believing in something you don't understand, but for which there is overwhelming evidence. Christian faith has stood the test of time and is well-described by that definition.

Starting with ancient civilizations, people have recognized the need to satisfy the spiritual or faith dimension of life. The proof of this comes from archaeological digs which uncover altars people used to worship their perceived gods. Many religions still try to fill that spiritual need experienced by people everywhere. And common to all religions—Christians, Buddhists, Hindus, Muslims and Jews alike—is the fact that there are many things about faith that can't be fully understood. But like electricity, ignition and milk, they're simply accepted as fact.

SO WHAT'S THE DIFFERENCE?

Some question why they should become Christians rather than join other religions. The big difference is that the others all require certain rules to be strictly followed and certain goals to be reached in order for people to have any chance of an afterlife. Contrary to the perception of some, Christianity has no requirements other than to admit that we are sinners and need to be forgiven by a loving God.

Christians believe that there is only one true God who has existed from before the beginning of time. He created the universe and governs all of human history. World and religious leaders come and go, but the same God still reigns over all. Nothing ever happens that surprises him, though he can be disappointed by decisions and choices made by those he created.

Christians also believe that in spite of our bad choices, our creator God loves us enough to send his son, Jesus, to die for sinners like us. Through faith in him, we experience his forgiveness. Christians believe that God's forgiving grace through Jesus is new every morning—the darkness of yesterday's sin is gone as surely as the darkness of night gives way to the light of a new day. That gives us purpose in living, and when we die, the promise of eternal life.

WHAT'S SO SPECIAL ABOUT A MAN NAMED JESUS?

Almost everyone has heard of Jesus. Some even use his name as profanity. Yet many don't really know much about him or understand his purpose. What makes Jesus any different than the prophets or leaders of other religions? To answer that question, think about what year it is right now. Approximately that many years ago, an incredibly powerful event took place that split time and dated all of human history. That event? Christmas happened! Jesus, the most influential person in all of history, was born—a birthday that has been celebrated every year all around the world ever since!

Though BC/AD may sound like a rock band's name, it is the widely accepted historical marker that divides human existence into BC (Before Christ) and AD (Anno Domini or "the Year of our Lord"). No other human being has ever had that kind of impact on history! Isn't it more than amazing that, of all the great people—kings, rulers, dictators, presidents and prophets—the world has ever known, only the brief life of a man named Jesus had the power to date history?

Jesus was a historical person, and his life is well documented. The son of a Jewish carpenter, he lived 33 years, and he was a public figure for just the last three years of his life. During that time, he taught a ragtag group of disciples about his purpose and performed many miracles of healing the sick among the crowds that followed him.

Many of his followers mistakenly thought he had come to set up an earthly kingdom. The Jewish elders falsely accused him of blasphemy. His short life ended when those charges were used by the Roman leaders to have him tortured and brutally crucified on a cross. Three days later, as he had predicted, he arose from the dead. That happened on Easter, which along with Christmas is still celebrated annually around the world.

Ron Ezinga

As has happened over time to other personality-dependent religious groups, Christianity should have died out when its leader died. Instead, it flourished and has become the predominant religion in the world. In three short years, this son of a carpenter changed the lives of millions who have claimed him as their Savior.

So here's a simple question that begs an answer: *What could be so unique about a man named Jesus that history is dated by his birth?* The answer is in the uniqueness of his purpose. *Jesus came to live and die for sinners like us, who through faith in him would have a purpose in this life and the promise and assurance of eternal life when we die.*

These Bible verses speak very clearly about why Jesus came:
Referring to Jesus, Titus 2:14 says: "He gave his life to free us from every kind of sin, to cleanse us, and to make us his very own people, totally committed to doing good deeds." That's our *purpose!*

John 3:16 says: "God loved the world so much that he gave his one and only Son so that everyone who believes in him will not perish but have eternal life." That's our *promise!*

And in Romans 8:1-2 we find these words: "So now there is no condemnation for those who belong to Christ Jesus. And because you belong to him, the power of his life-giving Spirit has freed you from the power of sin that leads to death." That's our *assurance!*

Only God's unconditional love for us, demonstrated by Jesus' death in our place, provides that unmerited and free eternal life insurance. But it only covers those who repent and put their faith in him. Think of all the kinds of expensive insurance people buy: life, health, long-term healthcare, disability, etc. Yet, when it comes to totally free eternal life insurance, many leave life without it. It's sad but true that for them, the name of Jesus is just a profane word. But for those who repent and accept God's premium-free eternal life insurance, that name is heaven's password. It is the name that dates human history and opens the door to heaven. Jesus is the name above all names.

THE BOTTOM LINE:

Many deny Jesus' purpose in dying, looking elsewhere for their purpose for living. But he came from heaven to earth to *tell* the world of God's love for sinners. Then he went to the cross where he died to *prove* God's love for sinners. And from the cross he went to the grave to *pay* the price of sin for those who confess them. He then left the grave and went back to heaven to *wait* for the forgiven to come and experience his love forever.

THE MOST IMPORTANT DAY OF YOUR LIFE!

The two most important days of life have been identified as the "day you were born" and the "day you figured out why." But there is a third, even more important day. That's the day you die and make a return trip to your original construction material—dust! All the other days of your life are meaningless if you haven't figured out how to die successfully. Psalm 90:12 gives us a clue to understanding how to die successfully: "Teach us to realize the brevity of life, so that we may grow in wisdom." This verse emphasizes two important points: the brevity of life and the need to live wisely.

LIFE IS 100% FATAL

Wise people don't waste time, treasure or talent during the brief time they have on this earth. Death is in your future sooner or later—the mortality rate of human beings is 100%. And death is no respecter of age. Obituaries are full of dead people, of which about 20% are under 70 years old. Regardless of your age, you'll likely find someone near your age in any obituary listing. Every breath you take is one closer to dying. God gave us our first breath when we were born and takes away our last when we die.

Leaving those morbid thoughts, if you're reading this, you are alive today, and every breath you take is a gift from God. How you came into existence doesn't matter. What does matter is that you're here by the divine plan and purpose of your creator God. In Ephesians 2:10, the Bible makes it very clear that God created us to do good things he planned for us long ago. This verse gives meaning and purpose to life rather than just existing a few years, dying and fading away into the great beyond.

The day you figure out why you're here is important but then comes the most important day of your life—the day you die. As important as it might be to discover how and why you were born, and what your purpose is in life, it is absolutely critical that you understand this one indisputable and all-important fact: *Where you go when you die does not depend on what you have or haven't done in life. It totally depends on what you believe the day you die!*

HEAVEN IS YOUR DESTINATION IF...

The death of loved ones often causes us to reflect on what really matters. People talk about "getting their life in order," which includes making a will or trust, making funeral arrangements, and getting right with family and friends. All of that pales in significance to getting right with God before you die. God *is* your creator and you *will* meet him when you die. And he *will* ask you, "Why should I allow you into heaven?" How will you answer? A few of the *wrong* answers are: I'm not perfect, but I've been a reasonably good person; I've treated others well; I volunteered a lot of time and gave a lot of money; I've gone to church quite regularly. Those answers won't open heaven's gates. The only *right* answer is this one: *I know that I'm a sinner, but I've confessed my sins, and Jesus has forgiven them.*

If you can't answer that way, be sure to read the upcoming page entitled "There are No Atheists in Foxholes." As long as you're alive, it's never too late and your sin is never too great. So why wait? Becoming a Christian is not a sign of weakness, rather a sign of strength for those who understand they can't make it on their own. The good news is that you don't have to catch up on your spiritual walk. You simply need to start walking with God now!

Though death is inevitable, it is not to be feared *if* you have signed up for God's free eternal life insurance. That can only be attained through repentance from your sin and placing your faith in Jesus who paid its premium with his life. For *all* who confess their sins and accept this gift of his amazing grace, God's eternal life insurance takes immediate effect. For them, the best is yet to come!

Ephesians 2:9-10 tells us that "Salvation is not a reward for the good things we have done, so none of us can boast about it. For we are God's masterpiece. He has created us anew in Christ Jesus, so we can do the good things he planned for us long ago."

Why You? *Because you are God's masterpiece!*

Why Here? *Because he has good things for you to do!*

Why Now? *Because he plans to give you hope and a future!*

Now What? *Live with purpose. Enjoy God's good gifts, but don't let your heart grow roots in the pleasures of the world. Share your gifts with him and others while serving him out of gratitude for his eternal love for you. And die with the promise of an eternity full of unending joy and blessing. That truly is masterpiece living!*

There Are No Atheists In Foxholes

This is an old military saying implying that when facing death on the battlefield, even atheists cry out to God for help. Of course, death can come at any time, so if you haven't secured God's free eternal life insurance, there's no time to waste. Take these steps to claim it:

1. **Believe that God has a purpose for your life.** In Jeremiah 29:11 God says: "I know the plans I have for you . . . plans for good . . . to give you a future." Ephesians 2:10 is even more specific: "We are God's masterpiece. He has created us anew in Christ Jesus, so we can do the good things he planned for us long ago."

2. **Confess that you are a sinner.** Romans 3:23 says it very plainly: "Everyone has sinned; we all fall short of God's glorious standard." Could you be guilty of: greed, impatience, jealousy, impure thoughts, or anger? You can probably think of a few more!

3. **Accept Jesus as your Savior.** Romans 5:8 says: "God showed his great love for us by sending Christ to die for us while we were still sinners." And Romans 10:13 says: "Everyone who calls on the name of the Lord will be saved."

If you have taken these three steps, confirm it with this prayer:

Dear God, thank you for your promise of eternal life possible only through Jesus' death. Though I don't understand it all, I believe that he died to pay for my sins which I confess right now. And I claim your promise that all my sins—past, present and future—have not only been forgiven but forgotten. Please fulfill your purpose for me, and help me live with gratitude, for Jesus' sake, Amen.

IT'S A NEW DAY!

If you prayed this prayer, Jesus says this to you in John 5:24: "Those who listen to my message and believe in God who sent me have eternal life. They will never be condemned for their sins . . . they have already passed from death to life." God's love for you is unconditional, and he is faithful to forgive those who trust him despite their failures. But, be aware that old Satan will do his best to convince you that you're too good or not good enough. So, to encourage you in your faith life, you should find a good church to attend to show gratitude for what Jesus has done for you.

To nurture that gratitude, begin each day with this brief prayer:

Dear God, thank you for this new day. Help me make it one that pleases you and blesses others. Thank you for your amazing love and forgiveness. Keep me in your will and way—today and every day—for Jesus' sake, Amen.

SECTION TWO

DEVELOP YOUR LIFE SKILLS

Contents

FEEL FREE TO COPY ANYTHING IN
THIS SECTION OR ANY PART OF
THE BOOK FOR PERSONAL USE.

Priming The Pump Of Life

This may be breaking news to younger generations, but water hasn't always come in bottles or even from a faucet! In the "good old days"—still true today in some developing countries—water came from wells. They were holes in the ground, dug by hand, from which water was drawn in buckets lowered into the hole on ropes.

Jump ahead a few years. A pipe was pounded down to the water table, and a pump was placed on the top of the pipe. Attached to the pump handle was a steel rod which went down into the pipe. Around that rod was a gasket which had to be made wet so that it would create a vacuum seal in the pipe, allowing water to be drawn up—literally sucked up—by the pumping action of the handle.

The simple process of wetting the gasket with water was called "priming the pump." Once primed, water flow was determined by the depth of the well and how vigorously one pumped the handle. You need to understand that much like the fact that cows don't *give* milk, wells don't *give* water. It has to be taken from both of them, often requiring the life skills of *patience* and *persistence!*

My experience with a pump—and milking cows—came in my preteen years when our family lived on a farm. When we first moved there, we didn't have running water in the house. So, at least once a day, water had to be hauled in with buckets filled from a pump which was out by the barn. That task often fell to me. On most summer days, the gasket in the pump would dry out between use, and the pump would need to be re-primed. I would dip some water from the adjacent livestock watering tank and pour it into the top of the pump, then quickly grab the handle and pump vigorously until the water started to flow. Once the flow started, there was no need to pump as hard. It only took steady pressure on the handle to keep water flowing. That was particularly helpful when that two hundred gallon livestock tank had to be pumped full on hot summer days!

What does the pump on a well have to say about life? Just as a pump needs the power of priming and pumping before it produces, we need the power of "primers" in our lives to be productive. Those primers come by way of our experiences, education, jobs, books, friends, family, churches and other positive influences in our lives. But, just as the pump wouldn't produce a *flow* of water without the pumping effort, the primers in our lives won't produce a *flow* of results without our effort to apply them. Without that persistent, steady effort, the *flow* in our lives will suffer.

LOOKING AHEAD

Zig Ziglar used to talk about the need to prime the pump of life—in order to get something out, you have to put something in first. The purpose of this section is to help you prime that pump of life so that, with a commitment to regular effort, your life can produce a steady flow of good results.

One challenge to getting those good results is learning how to deal with the negative issues we all face on a daily basis. In the following chapter, "Dealing with Life's Issues," you will learn how to keep negative issues from interfering with your ability to develop positive life skills that contribute to success in life.

Another challenge is that of maintaining balance in life. So the next chapter, "Developing Balance in Life," explains the multidimensional nature of human life, and introduces a unique tool called *LifeTrail* which can help you develop and maintain a balanced life.

Following those chapters, you will find actual *LifeSkillPrimers*. They will hopefully challenge, inspire and encourage you with topics that will positively affect your everyday life where the rubber meets the road. So, read on and you'll discover that the old pump out by the barn really does have a lot to say about *priming* the pump of life in a way that produces a steady *flow* of life skills which lead to masterpiece living!

DEALING WITH LIFE'S ISSUES

Is living successfully even possible in today's fallen world? The bad news is that there's a lot of junk out there which cause issues that can become very real obstacles to successful living. The good news is that, as you learned earlier, there are certain life skills that everyone can develop to deal with those issues while living a successful life.

An old children's song has these lyrics in it: "O be careful little eyes what you see" and "O be careful little ears what you hear." There's great wisdom in those few simple words because what we *see* and *hear* become *heart* issues in life. Proverbs 4:23 speaks very clearly to that danger: "Guard your heart above all else, for it determines the course of your life." It is very easy in today's world to let the pursuit of pleasure penetrate the defenses we should have around our hearts.

NO ONE'S PERFECT

Development of positive life skills will go a long way toward guarding our hearts, thereby determining the course of our lives. However, we know only too well the weaknesses of our human nature that we deal with every day. In other words, no one is perfect. That's a familiar statement made by many to justify or dismiss their wrong attitudes, words or deeds. But that statement is very true: no one is perfect, and that's why we have those issues in life.

The only humans who, for a very short time, didn't have issues in life were Adam and Eve. They were created perfect by God and placed in a tropical paradise. Talk about living a dream! But that dream soon became a nightmare when the devil, Satan, came calling. He convinced them that God really didn't mean it when he told them not to eat the fruit of one specific tree in the whole orchard. So, with all those beautiful trees loaded with luscious fruit which they were free to eat, they foolishly chose to listen to Satan and took a bite of that forbidden fruit. They had the original *ear, eye* and *heart* issues!

That terrible choice fractured their relationship with God, and their perfect world crashed in on them—and on us. Of course, they blamed Satan who—being a serpent—didn't have a leg to stand on! And from that day forward, "the devil made me do it" has been a popular rallying cry for all humanity seeking to avoid responsibility for their bad choices and actions.

But Adam and Eve's world-shaking disobedience, as well as that of all subsequent humanity, does *not* change the fact that God created us in his image. And, as distorted image-bearers, nothing has changed in our responsibility to live obediently according to God's principles. Knowing the challenge this is for us, the apostle Paul encourages us with these words in Ephesians 4:22-23: "Throw off . . . your former way of life . . . let the Spirit renew your thoughts and attitude."

A GREAT ATTITUDE

What does it mean to have your thoughts and attitude renewed? It can be argued that there are only two attitudes—*positive* and *negative.* If we are going to "throw off our former way of life" so we can deal with life's issues, it's critical to have a positive attitude. My friend and noted speaker Zig Ziglar claimed that the most important of all personal attributes or qualities is a positive attitude. Why? Because our minds are trained—positively or negatively—by our attitude. Practicing a positive attitude is of utmost importance in successfully dealing with life issues!

What are those issues and how does a positive attitude help in dealing with them? Look again at the list of desirable life skills that follow. Note that they are all actually positive attitudes which can become life skills through regular practice:

Confident   Considerate   Conscientious   Content   Decisive Dependable   Disciplined   Encouraging   Faithful   Forgiving   Friendly Generous   Honest   Humble   Industrious   Kind   Loyal   Optimistic Patient   Prompt

You will quickly discover that many of life's issues are actually the exact negative opposite of the positive life skills listed above: Faithful— *Unfaithful*, Friendly—*Grouchy*, Generous—*Selfish*, Humble—*Proud*, Industrious—*Lazy* and so on. Just these few examples illustrate serious life issues. Look again and you will discover that these life issues, stemming from the negative side of each life skill listed, are all evidence of attitude problems.

A negative attitude causes negative *life issues*—a positive attitude develops positive *life skills*. Simple as that! However, a positive attitude is not magic. It will not enable you to do things you're not capable of doing. But it will help you do what you are capable of doing better than a negative attitude will.

Struggling with attitude problems? Don't be discouraged. The struggle itself is a good sign that you're not giving up. We all experience attitude-affecting issues and challenges in life that require our perseverance. While we can't avoid them, we can choose our attitude in responding to them. A disciplined, positive attitude will go a long way toward dealing with life's issues, at the same time nurturing our life skills. It is a crucial ingredient in masterpiece living!

MAINTAINING LIFE BALANCE

Ask anyone what it means to be successful and they will usually equate success with money and possessions. Someone who lives in a large home with a luxury car or two in the garage, has a vacation home, plus all the expensive toys and trinkets, is automatically considered to be successful. However, being financially successful at doing something doesn't mean one is truly successful in life. There are a lot of miserable millionaires and bored billionaires who have a bunch of that stuff, yet their lives are empty and out of balance.

A DIRE WARNING

God warned about that emptiness in Deuteronomy 8:10-20 where he says: "Beware that in your plenty you do not forget the Lord your God and disobey his commands . . . for when you have become full and prosperous and have built fine homes to live in . . . and your silver and gold have multiplied along with everything else, be careful! Do not become proud at that time and forget the Lord your God . . . He is the one who gives you power to be successful . . . If you ever forget the Lord your God . . . you will certainly be destroyed."

No gray area there, right? The wealthy—by world standards, that's most people in developed countries—must not be prideful and take credit for their accomplishments. While God's warning is clear, what he doesn't say is also important. He doesn't condemn or criticize the wealthy. In fact, he takes credit for giving them the "power to be successful!"

Clearly, abundant material wealth does not automatically translate into a truly successful life. It can bring satisfaction and enjoyment into our lives, but it's only a form of failure if our priorities are wrong. Though the financial dimension is an important one, it needs to be in balance with other important priorities in life.

THE UNIQUENESS OF HUMANITY

One of the challenges we face in maintaining balance in our lives is our uniqueness. As opposed to other flesh and blood creatures, God created us as multidimensional beings with body, mind and spirit. In other words, we have *physical*, *mental* and *spiritual* dimensions to our lives. Without discipline—a word no one feels comfortable with—in maintaining a balance between life's dimensions, we will not be as effective in life as we could be. Our world of instant gratification is not a friend of a balanced life!

To understand the need for balance in life, think about your car. Besides filling the tank with the right type of fuel, its performance depends on regular maintenance and upkeep. If the tires are low on pressure and out of balance, they will wear out. A vehicle that is not cared for will sputter along until it finally breaks down completely. Our lives are much the same in their need for regular maintenance and the right fuel in our tanks if our lives are going to have the balance needed to succeed in all dimensions.

TOO MUCH TIME ON ONE DIMENSION?

Obviously, succeeding in one dimension of life at the expense of others is a problem. When a player on his team got four Fs and a D, Texas A&M basketball coach Shelby Metcalf told the young man, "Son, looks to me like you're spending too much time on one subject." In a humorous way, that clearly illustrates the very real danger we all face in maintaining balance in life.

To understand what is involved in our multidimensional existence, following are just a few of the aspects of life which fall under each dimension. While a case could be made for even more, you will notice two other very important dimensions of life—*relational* and *financial*—have been added to *physical, mental* and *spiritual*:

- **Physical:** Fitness, Nutrition, Recreation
- **Mental/Emotional:** Attitude, Habits, Thoughts
- **Spiritual:** Prayer, Worship, Devotions
- **Relational:** Marriage, Family, Friends
- **Financial:** Savings, Spending, Giving

At first glance, "daunting" may be the best word to describe the apparent challenge of this list. That might have been the word the young man in the earlier story would have used as he looked at all the classes he was expected to take in college. In fact, we would probably all agree that the expectations of coaches and parents, plus the effort needed to learn, was—and is—daunting for young people. They can't just focus on one subject and expect to succeed, so they do the best they can in all subjects and persevere.

Not much different than the challenges in all of daily life, right? It isn't just students who are faced with multiple expectations. As adults, we have to deal with the daunting complexity and busyness of our individual and family lives. Sometimes that results from unrealistic expectations placed on us by others, but we more often do it to ourselves. As a result, life is stress-filled with many ups and downs unless we can somehow gain control. The stress involved usually comes from being pressured by what Charles Hummel called the "tyranny of the urgent" rather than prioritizing the important.

THE MOST OVERLOOKED DIMENSION

A major risk in trying to live a balanced life is emphasizing some dimensions while neglecting others. And our human tendency is to spend too much time and effort on all dimensions except the *spiritual*. That dimension suffers because it doesn't appear on our daily must-do or want-to-do list where other fixed responsibilities like work and family appear. We always have time, or make time, for what we must do and want to do, right? Far too often, faith-building activities are not perceived as either, yet the foundation for success in *all* of life is the spiritual dimension!

Paul makes that crystal clear in 1 Timothy 4:8: "Physical training is good, but training for godliness is much better, promising benefits in this life and in the life to come." Physical training involves building muscle and strengthening the heart to help us live better and longer. But more importantly, our hearts—the most vital muscle in the body— must be strengthened spiritually for us to live forever. In other words, a strong physical heart will have benefits in this short life, but a heart strengthened by the grace of God is required for eternal life. It's critically important to get that spiritual dimension on our must-do list!

LIFE IS LIKE A MOUNTAIN TRAIL

Think about life in this scenario: Hiking a scenic trail up to soaring mountain peaks and back down through lush valleys can be exhilarating. But it's also exhausting. Not quite so exhilarating and even more exhausting are the peaks and valleys—the ups and downs—in real life. Like a tire that's badly out of round causes a car to shake until something eventually breaks, a life that's out of balance "shakes" until something eventually "breaks" in one dimension or another. And that results in chaos.

God has created us with unique personalities, interests and abilities, and he promises us the power to use and develop them. Our challenge is to use that power and our abilities to achieve balance between each of life's dimensions. To meet that challenge, you will find a unique tool called *LifeTrail* on the next page. It is a personal accountability tool to help you reach the sometimes exhilarating, often exhausting and usually elusive goal of maintaining balance in life. The same graphic along with instructions for using it are found on page 120 in the Life Skill Resources.

LifeTrail Accountability Tool

This unique tool can help you level out those hills and valleys in life. However, total objectivity is critical in recording where you are in each dimension. But remember . . . perfection is all 10s, which is impossible!

A	B	C	D	E
SPIRITUAL	PHYSICAL	MENTAL	RELATIONAL	FINANCIAL
Prayer	Fitness	Attitude	Marriage	Saving
Worship	Nutrition	Habits	Family	Spending
Devotions	Recreation	Thoughts	Friends	Giving

	A	B	C	D	E
10					
9					
8					
7					
6					
5					
4					
3					
2					
1					

FOUNDATION OF FAITH

Those who trust in the Lord will find new strength. They will soar high on wings like eagles.—Isaiah 40:31

God created us as multidimensional beings and all the dimensions are connected. When one suffers, they all suffer, so balance between each of those dimensions is the goal. You will discover that the higher and straighter your graph line is, the more content and happier you'll be!

LifeSkillPrimers
For Masterpiece Living

As illustrated by the story of the pump, our life skills need regular "priming and pumping" to produce a steady flow of positive results in our lives. That is the purpose of the *LifeSkillPrimers* (LSPs) in this section. They cover various topics that affect successful living either positively or negatively. They are brief, simple chapters which apply biblical principles to life in a very practical, common-sense way. Their purpose is threefold:

1. To help you develop successful life skills.
2. To encourage you in dealing with negative life issues.
3. To assist you in achieving that critical life balance.

Though these LSPs can be used individually, they are well-suited for use with another person or in a small group. For those involved, mutual encouragement and accountability are strong motivators to prime the pump of life. Since repetition is said to be the mother of learning, it is recommended that each chapter be read a few times during the week. You will note some duplication of content from the first section of the book, which is intended for emphasis of key points.

Each LSP encourages you to think about what you read under the heading "Learn, Obey, Confess or Celebrate." It is very easy to read something without really registering it in your mind. Jotting down some thoughts and impressions is a powerful way to help you be more aware of what you're reading. Of course, learning in any context is greatly enhanced by applying what is learned. So, for more in-depth study, you'll find corresponding Application Guides starting on page 126 in the Life Skill Resources.

To make *LifeSkillPrimers* even more effective in your life, be sure to regularly use the *LifeTrail* Accountability Tool found on page 121 of the Life Skill Resources. Finally, to carry with you as a reminder of the topic dealt with in each LSP, you will find *PocketPowerPrimers* starting on page 147 of the Life Skill Resources.

Copy and cut them often. Carry them with you and refer to them regularly to keep your "pump of life" primed. Share them with others to encourage them on their life's journey.

THE BOTTOM LINE:

The first section of this book will help you identify and develop life skills that enable you to better use your abilities. Conscientiously and consistently applying the *LifeSkillPrimers* in this section will result in your frustrations going down as your scores on *LifeTrail* go up.

LIFESKILLPRIMER TOPICS

This is a topical index of the *LifeSkillPrimers* that follow in the order listed. Note that they are grouped by three dimensions of our human existence: physical, mental and spiritual. Reminder: corresponding Application Guides can be found starting on page 126 in the Life Skill Resources.

PHYSICAL

Money: Root of Evil or Tree of Blessing?
Stewardship: Giving, Spending and Saving
Work: Therapy for Body and Soul
Goals and Priorities: Disciplines of a Successful Life
Integrity: A Legacy for Life
Rewarding Relationships
Marriage and Family: No Experience Required

MENTAL

The Power of a Positive Attitude
The Promise of Perseverance
Contentment: The Attitude of Gratitude
Habits: You Are What They Are
Choices: Planting Your Harvest
Pride and Jealousy: A Deadly Combination
Temptation: A Common Affliction

SPIRITUAL

God's Solution to Our Pollution
Forgiving Others Is Not Optional
The Fear Factor
Fact and Faith Fight Fear and Feelings
Prayer is Power
Church: Go or No?
Heaven: The "No More" Place

Money:
Root Of Evil Or Tree Of Blessing?

COMMON SENSE FROM THE BIBLE
"The generous will prosper. Those who refresh others will themselves be refreshed."—Proverbs 11:25

PRIMER POWER POINT
The love of money can get us in trouble. But through acts of generosity, money becomes a tree of blessing rather than the root of evil. Then we can enjoy the fruits of our labor while guarding our hearts from growing roots in the pleasures of the world.

The topic of money found its way into many of Jesus' conversations. In fact, many of his parables deal with money, as do many of the Proverbs. Why? Because money matters. It matters a lot! It makes the world go around, so to speak. Without money, no governments, schools, churches, ministries or any other entity you can name can exist. Neither can people!

Important as money is, the *love* of money can get us in trouble. In 1 Timothy 6:10, Paul warns against that problem, "For the love of money is the root of all kinds of evil." Many have used this verse to say that wealth is not a legitimate goal, but it's the *love* of money that is not legitimate. And in verse 17-18 of this chapter, Paul is very clear about the responsibility of those who are wealthy, "Teach those who are rich not to be proud and not to trust in their money . . . always being ready to share with others."

Rather than condemning the rich for their wealth, Paul is telling them to be willing to share the blessings God has provided. When sharing happens, rather than being the root of evil, money becomes a tree of great blessing—to those who share it and to those with whom it is shared.

Being willing to share with those who have less is a great responsibility for all citizens. That is especially true for citizens of God's kingdom who understand that abundant giving is an important key to abundant living.

The Bible has many more warnings to the rich about sharing their wealth. That's because having money and possessions can easily cloud our judgment and negatively affect our priorities if we're not careful. Possessions without priorities result in greed for more. The more we have, the easier it is to think that we did it on our own, so it's ours to do with as we please. In Matthew 6:21 Jesus said, "Wherever your treasure is, there the desires of your heart will also be." Our checkbooks provide a clear window into where our hearts are. How we spend money speaks volumes about what we feel is important in life. So it is true . . . money does talk!

Beatrice Kaufman said, "I've been rich and I've been poor and it's a whole lot better to be rich!" While most would quickly agree with that statement, there would be a huge difference of opinion on the definition of rich and poor. Consider the fact that almost everyone living in developed countries—even those below the poverty line in the U.S.—are rich compared to those struggling to survive in developing countries.

Admit it or not, most of us have more than we need, but often think we need more than we have. Jesus spoke about meeting our needs in Matthew 6:33 when he said, "Seek the kingdom of God above all else, and live righteously, and he will give you everything you need." Of course, that doesn't mean we simply sit and wait for dollars to fall from heaven. Seeking God's kingdom and living righteously implies a productive life of "doing good things he planned for us to do" as taught in Ephesians 2:10.

Life in most of the developed world is especially rewarding because of the free enterprise system. Long before any economists existed, the book of Proverbs was written. It teaches many of the key values of free enterprise such as integrity, hard work and profit. Those values rewarded many in biblical history, and they still do today. They encourage individual effort in using God-given abilities to achieve financial success.

If that describes you, beware of the danger that you love the gift and forget the giver. It is very easy to trust in money and possessions for security and forget God's provision of it. His instructions are the same today as they were to the Israelites before they entered the land of blessing he had promised them. In Deuteronomy 8:11 he said: "Beware that in your plenty you do not forget the Lord your God."

So enjoy the fruits of your labor, but don't let your heart grow roots in the pleasures of the world. Money can buy a piece of paradise on the beach, but it can't buy peace in God's paradise . . . that was purchased by Jesus at a price only he could pay!

Jot down your impressions from this Primer. Is there something
to: **LEARN, OBEY, CONFESS or CELEBRATE?**

_____

_____

_____

ON THE LIGHTER SIDE
Live within your means, even if you have to borrow to do it!

STEWARDSHIP:
GIVING, SAVING AND SPENDING

COMMON SENSE FROM THE BIBLE

"You must each decide in your heart how much to give. And don't give reluctantly or in response to pressure. 'For God loves a person who gives cheerfully.'"—2 Corinthians 9:7

PRIMER POWER POINT

In 2 Corinthians 8:12-13, Paul said: "Whatever you give is acceptable if you give it eagerly. And give according to what you have . . . of course, I don't mean your giving should make life easy for others and hard for yourselves."

Hoping to develop a sense of stewardship in his young son, a father gave him a quarter and a dime before going to church. He told him he could give whatever coin he wanted to church and spend the other one on himself. After church, the father eagerly asked what coin he had given. The lad thoughtfully replied that he knew the Lord loves a cheerful giver, and he could give the dime more cheerfully than the quarter. Lest you judge the lad too harshly, he actually gave almost 30% of the money he had. More of us should do that!

Seriously, stewardship involves much more than the financial dimension of life. There are four other important dimensions: spiritual, mental/emotional, financial and relational. But for our purposes here, we'll only look at the financial or material aspects of stewardship. Mark 10 records a conversation Jesus had with a rich man who had heard Jesus speak. He had sought Jesus out and asked him what he needed to do "to inherit eternal life." Jesus answered by reciting a short form of the Ten Commandments, to which the man replied that he had "obeyed all these commandments since I was young." Jesus then said, "There is still one thing you haven't done . . . sell all your possessions and give the money to the poor, and you will have treasure in heaven." The conversation ends with the man going away very sad because he had many possessions.

This person is symbolic of many in an affluent culture who live by the letter of the law, but whose possessions come first in their lives. He was concerned enough about eternal life to ask Jesus how to attain it, but his possessions were a higher priority to him. Jesus' challenge to this man is the same for us today. What are your priorities? Where is your trust? Jesus doesn't ask everyone to sell all their possessions—only those whose stuff stands in the way of trusting him.

That was the rich man's dilemma, and it's also yours if your trust is in your stuff. In that scenario, selling it may be the only way to have a relationship with Jesus in which you trust him for eternal life. Recently, a wealthy young Austrian man gave away his entire fortune because he came to the conclusion that it prevented him from experiencing genuine contentment. This principle is the same for all: No one will be truly content until they get what they need—a living relationship with Jesus!

The Merriam-Webster dictionary defines materialism as "a preoccupation with . . . material rather than spiritual or intellectual things." Sounds like that definition could have come from the Bible rather than the dictionary, right? A drive through any middle-class neighborhood would support that definition and reveal much about the importance of possessions to the occupants. Two-car garages, so full that there's no room for even one car, are probably a clue that all storage space in the house is full too. Not surprisingly, many of these same folks also have a full shed or barn in the backyard as well. And they might even be supporting the exploding self-storage rental business with stuff in one of them. Jesus might say much the same to these folks as he did to the rich man who walked away very sad.

As implied by the title page, there are three main ingredients in stewardship as it relates to life's financial dimension: giving, saving and spending. The order of those three words is significant to successful stewardship. If spending comes first, there will never be enough to save or give. There is never an easier time to give. If you wait until all that stuff in storage is paid for, giving ain't gonna happen! If giving is an afterthought, it will soon be a lost thought.

How does one decide how much is enough to give? A tithe (10%) of your income is a widely accepted minimum among Christians, but a more general principle is to give as you've prospered. Everything we have—our time, talents and treasure—is given to us by God, so the only thing we can give comes from what God first gave us. Be sure that if God's blessings have enabled you to raise your standard of living, he wants you to raise your standard of giving. A grateful heart is a giving heart, and abundant giving is the key to abundant living.

Jot down your impressions from this Primer. Is there something
to: **LEARN, OBEY, CONFESS or CELEBRATE?**

ON THE LIGHTER SIDE
"Don't steal—the government hates competition!"—Ron Paul

WORK:
THERAPY FOR BODY AND SOUL

COMMON SENSE FROM THE BIBLE
"There is nothing better than to enjoy food and drink and to find satisfaction in work . . . these pleasures are from the hand of God."—Ecclesiastes 2:24

PRIMER POWER POINT
A statement at the Franklin D. Roosevelt Memorial in Washington, D.C. brilliantly defines the importance of work: "No country, however rich, can afford the waste of its human resources. Demoralization caused by vast unemployment is our greatest extravagance. Morally, it is the greatest menace to our social order."

The statement found on the Roosevelt Memorial not only serves as a grim reminder of the Great Depression, it clearly illustrates the importance of work. One of the major decisions that pulled us out of that depression was to institute a public works program. Rather than sitting around with no income and mounting financial problems, people were put to work on public projects. The work gave them a feeling of accomplishment, and their pay gave them some financial stability. Not only did this program give many the experience and desire to get better jobs when the opportunity arose, it also provided motivation for improvement in other aspects of life.

Roosevelt's statement also has contemporary significance as a prophetic warning to any nation whose workforce is dwindling as a percentage of its population. It's also concerning when a large number of people in their prime working ages are not working. To paraphrase Roosevelt's warning, the waste of human resources is the greatest moral menace to social order.

Ron Ezinga

The Bible offers the solution to this problem in Ephesians 2:10: "We are God's masterpiece. He has created us anew in Christ Jesus, so we can do the good things he planned for us long ago." This should sound familiar since it has been a constant theme throughout this book. Our work or occupation is certainly an important part of the "good things" God planned for us to do. He provides for his world through the abilities he gives us and the work we do.

The importance of work is evidenced by it being one the most often used words in the Bible. For individuals, work produces income while providing a sense of purpose and fulfillment in life. For any society, the work of its citizens provides revenue to support government and other institutions which are needed for the common good.

Whatever our line of work is, it could—and should—be thought of as a calling. Too often, only work as preachers, teachers and other professionals is considered to be a "calling." But God has given each of us unique interests and abilities, which together contribute to the well-being of society. For example, what would the average hospital look like if there were doctors and nurses, but no janitors? After a few days, it could not function and there would be a very real risk of widespread infection and disease.

The example of the janitor's job illustrates its importance to a hospital or any other institution. But it is also instructive in understanding an individual's calling. Some people are janitors for life because they feel called to that occupation. Not only does the institution benefit from someone like that, so do the individuals with whom they have contact. A dedicated, outgoing janitor with a great attitude can have an uplifting effect on institutional morale. That doesn't mean that all janitors are called to that work for life. Those jobs might be stepping stones to other occupations. Then the attitude and people skills gained from their janitorial work contributes to their success at future jobs.

Interestingly, employers are more interested in a prospective employee's attitude than their skills. Proverbs 12:24 provides a basis for that interest:

"Work hard and become a leader." Those in any service industry who have positive attitudes towards work and customers quickly move ahead on their career path as they gain interpersonal skills that will easily transfer to any occupation. That probably isn't true for the burger flipper who, when asked, "How long have you worked here?" answered by saying, "Ever since the boss threatened to fire me!"

Our interests and abilities are important, but what's more important is what you do with them. God doesn't have regard for the prestige of our occupation. Rather, as is clear from Ephesians 6:7-8, he cares about the attitude with which our work is performed: "Work with enthusiasm, as though you were working for the Lord rather than for people. Remember that the Lord will reward each of us for the good we do." That is therapy for body and soul!

Jot down your impressions from this Primer. Is there something
to: **LEARN, OBEY, CONFESS or CELEBRATE?**

ON THE LIGHTER SIDE
Some people stop looking for work as soon as they get a job!
— Zig Ziglar

GOALS AND PRIORITIES:
DISCIPLINES OF A SUCCESSFUL LIFE

COMMON SENSE FROM THE BIBLE
"Good planning and hard work lead to prosperity, but hasty shortcuts lead to poverty."—Proverbs 21:5

PRIMER POWER POINT
Learn from these men. Solomon: "A dream fulfilled is a tree of life." Billy Graham: "Until a man gets his priorities in life straight, everything else is going to be out of order." Ben Franklin: "Motivation is when your dreams put on work clothes."

Have you ever set goals? For various reasons, talk about "goal setting" often intimidates us, even though most of us practice it almost daily. If that surprises you, think about your daily to-do list or weekly grocery lists. They actually represent goals that you set. Goal setting is nothing more than the process of planning to achieve something in the short, medium or long term. However, many goals are never achieved because they're not written down with a plan to achieve them. If you don't have a written to-do or grocery list, you will forget things you need to do or get.

An important key to successfully achieving goals is the ability to maintain needed priorities along the way. That process involves several life skills such as the need to be *persistent, decisive, motivated* and *self-controlled.* Together, goals and priorities become interdependent disciplines for a successful life.

Goals need to be specific, realistic and legitimate if there's to be any chance of reaching them. Wishing to climb Mt. Everest some day is not specific without a date, and it isn't realistic if you haven't trained properly. Also, for goals to be legitimate, they must fit into the priorities you should establish in each dimension of your life.

Success in reaching a goal is only another form of failure if your priorities are wrong. Billy Graham, the much-loved evangelist, said it this way: "Until a man gets his priorities in life straight, everything else is going to be out of order." A goal is a dream guided by a specific plan and reasonable priorities. Though you may have a dream or goal that fits those qualifications, achieving it will not just fall in your lap, even if it is supported by your God-given abilities.

Walt Disney said: "All our dreams can come true if we have the courage to pursue them." It's up to you to believe that you can do it, and you must be motivated to do the needed work. Without motivation, nothing gets started. Without work, nothing gets finished. There's truth in this old adage: "The harder you work, the luckier you get!"

While achieving goals provides direction and motivation for life, it's perfectly normal to lack motivation at times. When that happens, it's important to remember the benefits that motivated you to set that goal in the first place. Ben Franklin said: "Motivation is when your dreams put on work clothes." If you delay putting work clothes on your dreams, years will slip by, and you'll get caught up in the "if only I had done such and so" syndrome. Henry Ford came up with this deeply philosophical axiom: "If you keep doin' what you been doin' you'll keep gittin' what you been gittin'!"

Achieving short-term goals will provide a sense of accomplishment and the motivation to work on those of longer term. But daily demands on our time, real or perceived, can be overwhelming. Days seem too short to get everything done, and you freeze up mentally. That's normal too, especially if you have a mental to-do list rather than a prioritized written one.

Get that mental list on paper and it will be less intimidating and overwhelming. And do the most difficult thing on the list first. Think how satisfying it is to cross off everything on that list compared to a day when it seems you've accomplished nothing. That list contributed to your productivity and to your sense of well-being, especially if you handled the hardest thing first!

So how does one set goals and determine if they are realistic and legitimately fit into one's priorities? On page 123 of Life Skill Resources you'll find a very simple Goal Achievement Tool with suggestions. And on page 121 there is a copy of the *LifeTrail* Accountability Tool which can help you determine the legitimacy of goals. Together these tools will help you set and achieve goals within the right priorities that lead to a balanced, truly successful life. Reaching legitimate goals is extremely motivating and life-giving. That's what Solomon meant in Proverbs 13:12 where he wrote: "A dream fulfilled is a tree of life"

Jot down your impressions from this Primer. Is there something
to: **LEARN, OBEY, CONFESS or CELEBRATE?**

ON THE LIGHTER SIDE
"I started out with nothing. I still have most of it."—Michael Davis

INTEGRITY:
A LEGACY FOR LIFE

COMMON SENSE FROM THE BIBLE

"People with integrity walk safely, but those who follow crooked paths will slip and fall."—Proverbs 10:9

PRIMER POWER POINT

Integrity is a by-product of practicing the attributes God created in us. It defines the person who does the right thing even when no one is watching or in a position to know what was done. People of integrity leave a lasting legacy for everyone with whom they have contact, especially succeeding generations.

As a young college student working part-time at a local wholesale distributor, I had a unique opportunity to see what integrity looked like close-up. The owner of the company established his integrity with his customers and his employees quite unintentionally, yet very effectively. Here's how . . . wholesalers usually sell items to small retail stores in quantities of a dozen or more. Whenever the owner needed a pair of shoelaces or a toothbrush, he would go into the warehouse, open the box and take out one of what he needed. In its place, he put cash in the amount of the wholesale cost, usually a dollar or less.

As this became known to his customers and employees, they admired his honesty. They were impressed with the fact that, as the owner of the entire inventory, he could have taken a whole box of what he needed without paying anything, and no one would know the difference. You might say that's a small thing. But, as a man of integrity, he had learned a very simple lesson in life: If you cheat on small things, you're much more likely to cheat on larger things. His motto for life could well have been based on what Will Rogers once said: "You don't get a second chance to make a good first impression."

This man was a great example of someone who had learned the important life skill of *honesty* and practiced it even when no one was looking! As a result, his reputation for being fair and honest gave his employees and customers reason to trust him. Because of that trust and respect, both parties were much less likely to cheat him and were much more likely to be loyal customers and employees. A reputation for dishonesty would have had the very opposite, negative effect. He believed and lived out the teaching of Proverbs 22:1, "Choose a good reputation over great riches."

Written by Charles Reade, this metamorphosis of a life of integrity is a perfect fit with the philosophy of my former boss:

> Sow a thought and reap an act;
> Sow an act and reap a habit;
> Sow a habit and reap a character;
> Sow a character and reap a destiny.

A whole book could be written on these few words of wisdom, but it is quickly obvious that our destiny or legacy can be either a positive or negative one, depending on what type of thoughts begin the process. If one sows negative thoughts, there's no chance of reaping positive actions and habits. On the other hand, sowing positive thoughts will, in the end, reap a lasting legacy of *integrity*.

If you look back at that lengthy list of life skills (that you are hopefully practicing every day), you won't find integrity on it. That's because you become a person of integrity by developing life skills such as honesty, persistence, humility and courage. Those qualities are the ingredients in integrity. You won't find *reputation* or *character* on the list either for the same reason. Both are virtually interchangeable with integrity.

It would be nice to think that we are born with integrity, but babies aren't long in this world before they prove that to be fantasy. They quickly demonstrate the long reach of Adam and Eve's bad choice, and they provide indisputable proof that positive thoughts and actions don't come as standard equipment! Their young hearts need to develop an ability to know right from wrong, as well as the strength and courage to choose rightly between the two as they grow older and have to face a culture that often pushes us in wrong, godless ways.

Just as babies need guidance from loving parents to develop good thoughts, actions and habits, so we all need guidance from a loving God. He loves us so much that he planted his own attributes in us, and gave us the responsibility and the ability to develop them into life skills. Our integrity is a direct result of using those life skills to positively impact every dimension of our lives. That can only happen if we sow positive thoughts leading to the right actions, which then result in good habits, which develops strong character—all producing the legacy of a life of integrity!

Jot down your impressions from this Primer. Is there something
to: **LEARN, OBEY, CONFESS or CELEBRATE?**

ON THE LIGHTER SIDE
From a letter to the IRS: "I misrepresented my income and can't
sleep, so I have enclosed $150. If I still can't sleep, I'll send the rest."

REWARDING RELATIONSHIPS

COMMON SENSE FROM THE BIBLE

"Be humble, thinking of others as better than yourselves. Don't look out only for your own interests, but take an interest in others, too."—Philippians 2:3-4

PRIMER POWER POINT

In Matthew 7:12, Jesus stated what is widely known as the Golden Rule: "Do to others as you would like them to do to you." Just a simple smile or kind word, especially to those in need, encourages them today and brightens their tomorrows—and yours!

Did I do something for someone today? If you seriously consider that question, it could turn you and your normal day upside down! It is a question that has the potential for changing your life and the lives of others. "Paying it forward" is a popular phrase that implies doing something for someone that is totally unearned by that person because someone has done the same for you. Paul encourages us to do that when he challenged us to "take an interest in others." In our "me-first" world, Paul is warning against the sin of self-centeredness and encouraging us to be "others-oriented."

If we're honest with ourselves, we'd have to admit that our strong tendency is to think first of our own needs, often to the exclusion of those of others. For the very few individuals who are totally unselfish, their first concern is the welfare of others. That may be a natural inclination for those few, but the vast majority of us need to work hard to become others-oriented. That takes dedicated, conscious effort. Our natural instinct is to follow this infamous advice from Robert F. Kennedy: "Don't get mad, get even." That may satisfy a sense of self-preservation, but it does little to be others-oriented!

Every day of life is full of opportunities to encourage others in some way through random acts of kindness and concern. We simply need to be sensitive to those opportunities and have a willing spirit to respond to them. And when we encourage others and brighten their tomorrows by what we say and do today, it will brighten our own as well! It doesn't have to be much—offering a smile or friendly greeting to someone who appears to be discouraged, paying a few dollars for someone's groceries who may be in need, volunteering with a ministry to the underprivileged, or any other way you can "take an interest in others." Jesus was talking about that kind of thing in Matthew 25:40 (NIV) where he said: "Whatever you did for one of the least of these brothers and sisters of mine, you did for me." As difficult as that sometimes is, there are few things that are more rewarding—for both parties. And God will be glorified.

What about our more intimate, day-to-day relationships—those with family, friends and fellow workers? A smile or a kind word goes a long way there too. But Jesus implied even more in Matthew 7:12 where he stated what is widely known as the Golden Rule: "Do to others whatever you would like them to do to you." This means that you would treat others with the same concern and care that you desire from them. That's heavy stuff to think about and even more challenging to do!

A successful relationship is a two-way street. Again, because of our human tendency toward self-centeredness, deep-seated hurts can evolve over time that damage relationships, especially with those we love. We tend to judge others by their worst actions and ourselves by our best intentions. We struggle with our own faults even while we can't overlook those of others. The reverse of that is the solution: Overlooking the faults of others will help us overcome our own.

Even though there may be difficulties with loved ones at times, there probably are also special activities or events that provide good memories. What we remember affects our attitude and how we interact with them. We can't let today's challenges rob tomorrow of the good memories experienced in life's yesterdays. Here's a suggestion that, if practiced, could provide helpful therapy in dealing with difficult relationships, current or past: Remember the best, forget the rest. Actually, the word *forgive* should be added because there's no forgetting without first forgiving. Maybe this could be called the Silver Rule: "Remember the best—forgive and forget the rest!"

A forgiving heart is one which not only feels the hurt caused *by* others, but also one that is aware of the hurt caused *to* others. Though we need to forgive others for the hurt caused us, we should never forget what we learned from it. We must understand how we have offended God and how much he has unconditionally forgiven us. His grace can't find us if we're hiding behind a grudge!

Jot down your impressions from this Primer. Is there something to: **LEARN, OBEY, CONFESS or CELEBRATE?**

ON THE LIGHTER SIDE
"Happiness is good health and a bad memory."—Ingrid Bergman

Marriage And Family:
No Experience Needed

COMMON SENSE FROM THE BIBLE

"Give honor to marriage, and remain faithful to one another in marriage."—Hebrews 13:4

PRIMER POWER POINT

Stranger than fiction: What lifelong commitment would anyone in their right mind ever make without learning what is required by that commitment or being trained to perform all the requirements of it? It's called getting married and raising a family!

More than amazing, isn't it, that the world's two most critically important cultural institutions—marriage and parenting—require no training? "On-the-job" training has benefits in many situations but not so much in family love and care. That training deficiency shows up in the 50% divorce rate, and in the subsequent trauma for the affected families, especially the children. Very simply, that is not what God planned for those he created as masterpieces in his own image.

Going all the way back to our perfect parents in paradise, trouble started over eating some fruit. What could be a simpler decision than what kind of fruit to have for lunch, especially when God had told them what fruit was *not* on the menu? They ate the forbidden fruit and right there in paradise is where the blame game started. It is a "game" that everyone quickly learns to play—a game no one has ever won. You may get the last word but it's rarely a winning one, unless it is "sorry"!

There are many reasons for failed marriages, but the bottom line is usually selfish pride and a lack of forgiveness, which go hand in hand. In most of those divorces, research shows that second and third marriages are even less successful. Changing partners is not the answer; changing attitudes is. God intended for marriage to be a place of blessings, not a battlefield where petty peeves are allowed to play out. Marriage is not a 50-50 arrangement; rather it is a 100-100 deal where each spouse gives 100 percent. Anything less than that provides an opportunity for difficulties.

All marriages have rough spots in them. Don't ever believe anyone who says they have never had a disagreement with their spouse. If they'll lie about that, they'll lie about other things! I had the privilege of serving as an elder in a church we attended. There were many blessings but also frustrations involved in doing that work. Most frustrating was working with two couples at different times who were moving ahead with divorce plans.

When my elder partner and I asked them why they were pursuing this action, both couples replied that when they looked around in church, they saw everyone smiling and seemingly happy. They felt they were the only ones who were experiencing difficulties in their marriages. We assured them that all marriages had rocky spots, including our own. Sadly, both couples went through with their divorces.

A strong marriage usually translates into a strong family. That can't happen unless both partners are on the same page, and they can't be on the same page if there's constant turmoil and tension. If only we could live in the awareness that we—as individuals, as married couples and as families—were all God's idea. As Ephesians 2:10 tells us, he not only created us in his image as his masterpieces, he also planned good things for us to do. No doubt a strong marriage and family are included in those good things he planned for us. What an awesome opportunity—and responsibility!

Just think about the miracle a married couple is involved in if they are blessed with children. They have the opportunity to partner with God in perpetuating humanity during the nine months before childbirth.

Then they have the responsibility of providing a stable marriage and home environment for their children. Since children learn more by seeing than listening, a huge part of that environment is being genuine life examples for the kids. No doubt there'll be times when that example isn't God-like, but kids will then learn about the need for apology and forgiveness.

Hebrews 13:4 began this *LifeSkillPrimer* with these words: "Give honor to marriage, and remain faithful to one another in marriage." That simple guideline implies the need for all the ingredients that go into fulfilling it, such as mutual respect and trust, love for—and submission to—each other, goals and expectations that are openly and honestly agreed on, and more.

Of course, the strongest undergirding foundation of marriage is a mutual faith in Almighty God who in his providence brought together two lovestruck individuals to do those good things he planned for them long ago!

Jot down your impressions from this Primer. Is there something
to: **LEARN, OBEY, CONFESS or CELEBRATE?**

_____

_____

_____

ON THE LIGHTER SIDE
Parents watch their daughter marry a man who isn't nearly
good enough for her, hoping there will be grandchildren
who are smarter and better looking than anyone else's!

THE POWER OF A POSITIVE ATTITUDE

COMMON SENSE FROM THE BIBLE
Fix your thoughts on what is true, and honorable, and right, and pure, and lovely, and admirable. Think about things that are excellent and worthy of praise.—Philippians 4:8

PRIMER POWER POINT
The mind can be used for both good and evil. As humans, we tend toward evil. A powerful weapon for combatting that tendency is a positive attitude, which is life-healing, while a negative attitude is life-hardening. Both are extremely contagious!

In the early 1940s, Johnny Mercer made a song popular which repeated these lyrics: "You got to accentuate the positive, eliminate the negative." While our world churns around us, as it has since the beginning of time, accentuating the positive can be a real challenge. Add our own personal or family challenges to the world mess, and we can easily succumb to the negative.

Though the words "positive attitude" may not appear in Bible, there is a great deal of emphasis on positive living. Charles Swindoll, who has written much on the topic, believes Philippians 4:8 is the scriptural foundation for a positive attitude. It tells us to think about things that are excellent and worthy of praise such as what is true, honorable, right, pure, lovely and admirable.

What kind of "excellent things" was Paul referring to in that verse? He was probably referring to the "fruits of the Spirit" he wrote about in Galatians 5:22-23: "The Holy Spirit produces this kind of fruit in our lives: love, joy, peace, patience, kindness, goodness, faithfulness, gentleness, and self-control." All very positive qualities, right? Actually, if you look closely, these are all attitudes—very positive attitudes. There's nothing negative about any of them. And they are attitudes which can become skills if practiced as Paul recommended.

Proverbs virtually overflows with the results of practicing these attitudes. Here are just a few: "The lips of the godly speak helpful words" (10:32). "An encouraging word cheers a person up" (12:25). "A peaceful heart leads to a healthy body" (14:30). "A glad heart makes a happy face" (15:13). "The path of life leads upward for the wise" (15:24). "The king is pleased with words from righteous lips; he loves those who speak honestly" (16:13). "Love prospers when a fault is forgiven" (17:9). "A cheerful heart is good medicine" (17:22). A positive attitude is one of the most important life skills anyone can develop to be successful in life.

My friend Zig Ziglar used this simple example that clearly shows the power of a positive attitude: Think about your attitude the day before you go on vacation. Positive and excited, right? Are you able to get a whole bunch more accomplished that day—at home or work—than compared to normal days? Of course! Are you any smarter or stronger that day? Of course not! The only difference was your mental attitude. It motivated you to get everything done that needed doing before you left on vacation.

So the secret to your being more positive and productive is more vacations, right? Probably not, but this example does illustrate how a positive attitude can be an important contributor to success. However, being positive doesn't come naturally to most of us—it's much easier to think negatively. We have been conditioned to negativity by our culture, and often by those around us, even other Christians at times. Television newscasts regularly focus on the negative. Some movies, TV programs, video games and other forms of entertainment infect our culture with violence and many forms of immoral behavior.

Combating all that negativity requires a powerful weapon, which is the mind. Buddha is said to have made this statement: "The mind is everything. What you think, you become." Paul wrote this in Ephesians 4:22-23 (NIV): "You were taught . . . to be made new in the attitude of your minds." Similarly, the apostle Peter wrote in 1 Peter 1:13 (NIV): "Prepare your minds for action." Buddha, Paul and Peter are all on the same page in challenging us to practice a positive mental attitude regardless of our circumstances. Right thoughts produce right actions.

Don't get discouraged—good changes take time. We all experience difficulties and challenges in life. We can't avoid them, but we can choose our attitude toward them. Peter, Paul and yes, Buddha, would probably all agree that a positive attitude is life-healing and a negative attitude is life-hardening. Both are extremely contagious!

Jot down your impressions from this Primer. Is there something
to: **LEARN, OBEY, CONFESS or CELEBRATE?**

_____

_____

_____

ON THE LIGHTER SIDE
"Always borrow money from a pessimist. He
won't expect it back."—Oscar Wilde

THE PROMISE OF PERSEVERANCE

COMMON SENSE FROM THE BIBLE

"Whoever pursues righteousness and love finds life, prosperity, and honor."—Proverbs 21:21 (NIV)

PRIMER POWER POINT

There's a close connection between perseverance and our abilities. Perseverance is a life skill which unlocks and enables the abilities God has entrusted to each of us. We become what he intended us to be through persevering in using those abilities.

To pursue is synonymous with perseverance, which is a big word that simply means "keep on keeping on" through whatever obstacles come your way. Mr. Webster's dictionary defines perseverance this way: "Continued effort to do or achieve something despite difficulties, failure, or opposition." The operative word in that definition is difficulties. Without difficulties, it's easy to persevere in life, but real life is never without difficulties. Accidents, health issues, family challenges, job loss and other obstacles are a very real part of life for all of us. And they can be stepping stones to reaching God's purpose for us—not reasons for failure.

Volumes have been written on dealing with life's challenges. For people of faith, the bottom line is always that God is in control and knows everything about what we're going through. All we need to do is trust him. But that can often make the struggle even more difficult, because in those excruciating times, trust often borders on terror. Religious platitudes do little to ease our pain at such times and can cause resentment against God and others. The struggle is sometimes overwhelming! Though we know we should pray, our feeble attempts seem hollow and empty. Yet there's much to be gained through the act of prayer, since crying out to God for his help in our helplessness strengthens us emotionally and spiritually.

To persevere in those times, about all we can do is hang on—as if by our fingernails—to what we know to be true: that God is our refuge and he does care. Though seemingly fragile, that kind of "fingernail perseverance" is like a small anchor holding a large ship in raging seas. It takes sheer determination, but it will hold us until the storm in our sea of life subside and the rays of God's love break through what seemed to be permanently dark storm clouds. The Christian life is like a foot race that requires perseverance and endurance. Hebrews 12:1-3 (NIV) talks about that race: "Let us run with perseverance the race marked out for us . . . fixing our eyes on Jesus . . . so that you will not grow weary and lose heart."

Perseverance is an important life skill that needs to be developed in all the dimensions of everyday living—physical, spiritual, mental, relational and financial. There is a certain amount (often a lot) of drudgery in every marriage, family, career, friendship and financial situation, as well as in the daily grind of life that requires us to persevere if we want to succeed in those areas. Feelings of frustration often make us question whether it's even worth the struggle. But that's what it often takes to resolve difficult situations. So, keep on—keeping on.

Proverbs 21:21 makes it clear that perseverance is worth the effort. "Life, prosperity and honor" result from pursuing righteousness and love. Much of the drudgery and most of the frustrations in life can be overcome by righteousness and love. But, like eating and bathing, they need to be practiced regularly to be effective. Our perseverance unlocks the abilities God has entrusted to each of us, and we become what God intended us to be through the use of those abilities.

The connection between perseverance and abilities is clear in an interesting story Jesus tells in Matthew 25:14-30 about a wealthy man who entrusted his money to his three servants before he left on a long trip. He divided the money "in proportion to their abilities," giving one servant five bags of silver, two bags to the second and one bag to the third. When he returned from his trip, the master called for an accounting of how the servants had handled his money. The first servant reported that he had doubled his five bags; the second had also doubled his two bags; but the third said he had buried his only bag to preserve the master's money.

Of course, the master was elated with the results of the first two servants, so he rewarded their perseverance with promotions and a party in their honor. The third servant was chastised for being too lazy to even put his money in the bank where it could at least earn interest. Are you using the abilities the God gave you or are you burying them? If we persevere in using them as two servants did, we can expect God's blessing on our efforts. That's the *promise of perseverance!*

Jot down your impressions from this Primer. Is there something
to: **LEARN, OBEY, CONFESS or CELEBRATE?**

_____

_____

_____

ON THE LIGHTER SIDE
"By perseverance the snail reached the ark."—Charles Spurgeon
They never gave up so . . . get up and never, ever give up!

CONTENTMENT:
THE ATTITUDE OF GRATITUDE

COMMON SENSE FROM THE BIBLE

I have learned in whatever state I am, to be content.—Philippians 4:11 (NKJV)

PRIMERPOWERPOINT

Our contentment should never depend on our comfortable circumstances, material possessions or freedom from pain or sorrow. Rather, it must come from gratitude to God for our relationship with him, trusting him for what we need—not what we want.

Zig Ziglar was fond of saying that the text above proves that the apostle Paul was not a Texan. Why? Because no true Texan would be content in any other state! Of course, Paul was not talking about a geographical state; rather, he was talking about a condition or state of mind. No doubt he would agree that contentment comes from a confidence that nothing happens outside of God's will and control.

It is interesting that he would say he "learned" how to be content. That implies that he wasn't content at one time, but now has learned how, in spite of being beaten, shipwrecked or jailed, which is where he was when he wrote this! We don't have to go to jail to learn or prove our contentment just because Paul did. No doubt, he received special grace from God to endure all that he encountered in life. But, as he did for Paul, God does promise us grace sufficient to our needs, too. We've all experienced that life is like a pendulum, swinging from joy to sorrow, from contentment to apprehension.

So, the question is, does "contented" describe your normal state of mind? Just as it was for Paul, contentment is a learned attitude and is one of those life skills you are hopefully practicing. No one can be content 100% of the time. But if discontent describes your usual feelings, there's work to do! Contentment is found in getting what we need rather than more of what we want but don't need. In other words, it is found in realizing how much you already have and trusting God for his provision for what we might lack.

Jesus told an interesting story in Luke 12:16-21 about how a rich farmer tried to find contentment. This wealthy man owned very fertile land that produced such huge harvests that he didn't have room in his barns to store it all. So he decided to tear them down and build bigger barns. That way, he reasoned, he'd have enough stored away for years to come. Then he could kick back and eat, drink and be happy! That night he died, and all of his wealth went to others. Jesus concluded this story by saying: "A person is a fool to store up earthly wealth but not have a rich relationship with God." This story implies that this rich farmer had the wrong priorities. He had stuff that gave him temporary happiness, but his source of lasting contentment was not in his relationship with God.

It would be normal at this point to wonder if it's wrong to have "full barns?" Proverbs 3:7-10 (NIV) puts this question in the right perspective: "Do not be wise in your own eyes; fear the Lord and shun evil. This will bring health to your body . . . honor the Lord with your wealth . . . then your barns will be filled to overflowing." So, overflowing barns could be a blessing from God if we're in the right relationship with him. But, as indicated by the story of the rich farmer, contentment does not come from barns full of stuff. In fact, it is true for many that the more stuff they have, the more they want, and the less content they are. A living relationship with God is what we all need—then we can be more content with what we have!

Just like Paul, we have to learn how to be content in our circumstances. And there's one word that is key to learning contentment: gratitude. It has been said that gratitude is made up of two words: GReat ATTITUDE.

Makes sense, doesn't it? A good way to practice gratitude—a great attitude—is to be thankful for what you have rather than focus on what you think you lack.

In 1 Thessalonians 5:18, the same apostle Paul who had to learn to be content in all circumstances gave us this sage advice: "Be thankful in all circumstances." But what he did *not* say is important—he did not say to be thankful *for* all circumstances. If your house burns down along with all your stuff in it, God doesn't expect you to thank him *for* that. But he wants us to be grateful that, among other things, no lives were lost, insurance will cover most of the loss, and through the combination of your persistence and his provision, you can survive and rebuild for an even better future.

An attitude of gratitude is a powerful tool for practicing the life skill of *contentment,* even in life's most dire circumstances!

_____

Jot down your impressions from this Primer. Is there something
to: **LEARN, OBEY, CONFESS or CELEBRATE?**

_____

_____

_____

ON THE LIGHTER SIDE
Junk is something you throw away three weeks before you need it!

HABITS:
YOU ARE WHAT THEY ARE

COMMON SENSE FROM THE BIBLE

"I have discovered this principle of life—that when I want to do what is right, I inevitably do what is wrong."—Romans 7:21

PRIMER POWER POINT

Edmund Burke said that "those who don't know history are destined to repeat it." Though that was said in a national context, there is great wisdom in applying that statement to individual human life as it relates to learning from our habits—good or bad.

"When I want to do what is right, I inevitably do what is wrong." It is amazing that this statement was made by the apostle Paul! If he, who was a pillar in the early church, made a statement like that, what chance do we ordinary people have? Actually, we have the same chance Paul had, since he was as human as we are. As we do today, all the so-called heroes of faith struggled with the same tendencies. We all want to do what is right, yet the human tendency is always within us to do what's wrong. And that's where habits come into play. If we don't fight that tendency, the results show up in our habits.

Habits, good and bad, influence our daily choices and decisions. To illustrate that, let's take a quick look at how habits relate to each of the five dimensions of human life identified earlier in this book:

- *Physical:* Regular exercise is a good habit—no exercise is bad.
- *Mental:* Being positive is a good habit—being negative is bad.
- *Spiritual:* Praying is a good habit—not praying is bad.

- *Relational:* Being friendly is a good habit—being a grouch is bad.
- *Financial:* Saving money is a good habit—not saving is bad.

Habits define us and are developed by what we do regularly. Will Durant summed up Aristotle's words by saying: "We are what we repeatedly do." "Repeatedly" is the operative word because doing something once in a while does not constitute a habit. However, doing the wrong thing once in a while has a—here's that word again—tendency to become a bad habit much more quickly than doing the right thing once in a while becomes a good one.

Once bad habits take hold, changing them can be excruciatingly difficult, even if you know what you are doing wrong. Professional athletes sometimes develop bad habits in their "mechanics." Very quickly, a star athlete becomes ordinary. At that point, even though they know what they're doing is wrong, doing it correctly seems strange until regular practice of the correct way restores their ability once more.

Bad habits in life are no different. Somehow our "mechanics" can get messed up from what we know they should be. We become comfortable with bad habits, and eliminating them can be traumatic. People who developed a smoking habit know how traumatic it is to quit! Addictive habits are so debilitating because the pattern of addictive thoughts overwhelm any efforts to change. To a greater or lesser degree, that applies to other bad habits, such as being critical, sarcastic, impatient and all sorts of wrong tendencies we have. It takes enormous effort to change a bad habit, but it can be done through regular practice.

Good habits give life order and structure. Bad habits do the opposite. In the absence of good habits to replace them, bad habits always take up all the "space" available. Habits become a matter of motivation and who you are serving. The lyrics in one of Bob Dylan's songs says: "It may be the devil or it may be the Lord but you're gonna have to serve somebody." The only solution to bad habits may require a change in who you're serving, as Dylan said—the devil or the Lord!

While most would not say they want to serve the devil, it's sad that many don't see that as a choice to be made with any urgency. But Dylan's song was absolutely right—the devil or the Lord are the only two choices available. If you don't choose the Lord, you're choosing the devil by default. And that old devil Satan loves to have people in that vulnerable position!

The apostle Paul, who admitted to his struggle with doing right and wrong, also said this in 2 Corinthians 5:17: "Anyone who belongs to Christ has become a new person. The old life is gone; a new life has begun!" That doesn't mean that new life will be easy because, as we've seen, old habits are difficult to break. We'll still struggle with those old tendencies and habits. But through choosing to serve the Lord rather than the devil, and by replacing bad habits with solid life skills, we can get our life's "mechanics" back to where they need to be. Only then can we become what God intended, his masterpieces recreated in Jesus to do "good things he planned for us long ago!"

Jot down your impressions from this Primer. Is there something
_to:_ **LEARN, OBEY, CONFESS or CELEBRATE?**

_____

_____

_____

ON THE LIGHTER SIDE
"Time you enjoy wasting is not wasted time."—Bertrand Russell

CHOICES:
PLANTING YOUR HARVEST

COMMON SENSE FROM THE BIBLE
"Don't be misled . . . You will always harvest what you plant. Those who live only to satisfy their own sinful nature will harvest decay and death . . . So let's not get tired of doing what is good. At just the right time we will reap a harvest of blessing if we don't give up."—Galatians 6:7-9

PRIMER POWER POINT
Starting with the world's first family, history is filled with ruined lives due to bad choices. Watch the news and you'll see lives of politicians and celebrities implode in living color! Unbelievable? Be careful—none of us are immune to making bad choices.

It's all Adam and Eve's fault, right? They had it made in paradise until Satan came around. And they believed him rather than God, who had forbidden them to eat from just one tree out of all the trees loaded with fruit. They chose to disobey and spoiled it for all of us. Actually, the story in the Bible seems to indicate that Eve was the one who took the first bite of the fruit. This scenario gives some credence to a rather humorous story that you won't find in the Bible.

The story has Adam and his two boys walking past the entrance to the paradise from which they had earlier been expelled because of their choice to eat the forbidden fruit. God had placed a flaming sword at the gate to keep anyone from entering. Of course, boys will be boys, and Adam's boys were intrigued by that sword, so they had to take a closer look. While Adam was preoccupied with surfing the web on his cell phone, one of the boys peeked inside the gate and was awestruck by the beauty. He exclaimed, "Daddy, what in the world is that beautiful place?" Reportedly, Adam's reply was, "That's where your momma ate us out of house and home!"

While the validity of that story is questionable at best, the choice Adam and Eve made did have disastrous results for the entire human race. They chose death rather than life, poverty rather than prosperity. Their choice brought sin into the world for the first time, and it has infected everyone born since. Choosing to violate God's boundaries and to do it our own way is a natural tendency that runs rampant in every institution of society. We need the protective boundaries God puts in place for our good. We are happiest when we know where the boundaries are and then live within them.

It's like the new school that was built. Initially there was no fence around the playground. When the kids went out for recess and after lunch, they mostly just huddled in the middle of the playground. But when the fence was finally built, the children spread out and enjoyed playing games and running around much more freely than before. The fence was a protective boundary which gave them a greater sense of freedom and security. Observing God's boundaries and choosing to live within them does the same for us, making life more enjoyable.

In the game of golf, there are penalties for going out of bounds. No serious golfer chooses to hit their ball out of bounds. In real life, choosing to go outside the boundaries leads to all kinds of problems. Yet that is our tendency. Poor choices are always predictors of problems in the future. In other words, our future depends on today's choices. And the choices we make affect not only our own lives, but also the lives of others. It's really sad to watch people's lives—often the lives of loved ones—implode due to bad choices.

It's only natural to wonder why God doesn't prevent us from making bad choices. It's because he didn't create us as robots that he could operate remotely. He gave us rational minds and free wills to make our own decisions. Does being a Christian make choices easier? It probably should, but good choices are even more challenging for Christians in a permissive culture that ridicules traditional values and trivializes the importance of faith. And because of negative peer pressure, good choices are especially challenging for Christians if they are the only ones in a group making the right choice. When faced with a choice you find difficult to make, ask yourself: *What does God desire for me?* That short question quickly clarifies the right choice!

The good news is that our poor choices—along with other sins—are covered by a choice Jesus made. As the only sinless human being who ever lived, Jesus was the only one who could pay for sin. He chose to sacrifice his life on the cross to cover Adam and Eve's disastrous choice and our bad choices ever since. That was the choice of all choices—a sin-shattering and life-giving one! His sacrifice provides the only way for us to deal with our sins of the past, and gives us the power to get it right in the future.

Jot down your impressions from this Primer. Is there something
to: **LEARN, OBEY, CONFESS or CELEBRATE?**

_____

_____

_____

ON THE LIGHTER SIDE
The choice of a nursing home in your future may be made by
someone else . . . be really nice to anyone that might be!

PRIDE AND JEALOUSY:
A DEADLY COMBINATION

COMMON SENSE FROM THE BIBLE
"God opposes the proud but favors the humble . . . humble yourself before the Lord and he will lift you up in honor."—James 4:6-10

PRIMER POWER POINT
Like any other human failing, pride is not an unforgivable sin. It is simply more evidence of our need for God's forgiveness, which he promises if we repent. Of course, God doesn't honor our sin, but he does honor our humble repentance.

A sign along the highway has this thought-provoking statement: "Too much humility is really pride." Is it really possible to have too much humility? If you're the only one who thinks you're too humble, it certainly is! There's a fine line between humility and pride that is so easily crossed, even by Christians. If you're proud of being humble, you have definitely crossed that line! C. S. Lewis said: "Humility is not thinking less of yourself, it is thinking of yourself less."

Pride is a close cousin to jealousy, and when they, along with anger, coexist in a human being, things can turn deadly. In fact, according to Genesis 4, we find that the first family experienced exactly that. Cain and Able brought offerings to God. God looked with favor on Abel's offering but not Cain's. We're not told why that was, but because of it, Cain became extremely angry and jealous. His selfish pride was probably the root cause of his problem.

God provides a strong warning for all of us when he responds to Cain's anger, saying to him, "Why are so you angry? You will be accepted if you do what is right. But if you refuse to do what is right, then watch out! Sin is crouching at the door; eager to control you. But you must subdue it and be its master." The next thing we read is that Cain invites Abel to go for a walk in the field where he brutally murders him.

Everyone has heard the old saying "Pride goes before the fall," which is a paraphrase of Proverbs 16:18. That's as true today as ever. Just look at those in the political, entertainment, sports and, yes, even religious arenas of life. You'll find many examples of prominent people whose pride preceded very humiliating falls from positions of respect, power, fame and fortune. And their credibility is completely destroyed.

Pride is probably the most common of all sins that we need to confess on a regular basis. Pride has been described as being puffed up, overbearing and boastful. Do you know anyone like that? Careful now—when you point a finger at someone else, there are three fingers pointing back at you! Humility is a very critical and powerful life skill that takes constant effort to achieve.

So where's the line between pride and humility? There is such a thing as legitimate pride in achievements, but even that can be dangerous. God created us with certain abilities and talents. Not using them would dishonor him, while using them in the right way brings glory to him. If the way you relate your achievements to others brings glory to God, it's humility. If it brings glory to you, it's pride. That's the line!

Pride is closely tied to another issue of our humanity, which is peer pressure. It afflicts all ages, not just teens. Peer pressure can be positive, but is often negative, leading to doing the wrong things out of pride. Pride makes us want to be part of the crowd, which is most often not where we should be. Succumbing to negative peer pressure results from our pride and the fear of humiliation.

Regardless of our age, we all want to be recognized for who we are and what we do. There's something in our human DNA that creates a desire to be recognized for the good we do. If sincere peer recognition and encouragement comes, be thankful, but be careful that it doesn't feed a prideful desire for even more praise. When there is no public recognition, remember that God does see everything. And he rewards us for those things done out of humility that honor him. Proverbs 22:4 says it well: "True humility and fear of the Lord lead to riches, honor, and a long life."

No one has ever been more humble than Jesus, yet no one has ever been more humiliated. His friends deserted him when he needed them most. He was insulted, beaten and hung on a cruel cross where he was ridiculed until his lifeblood ran out. And he did it for you and me!

Jot down your impressions from this Primer. Is there something
to: **LEARN, OBEY, CONFESS or CELEBRATE?**

_____

_____

_____

ON THE LIGHTER SIDE
"Humility is like underwear; essential, but
indecent if it shows!"—Helen Nielsen

TEMPTATION:
A COMMON AFFLICTION

COMMON SENSE FROM THE BIBLE

"The temptations in your life are no different from what others experience. And God is faithful. He will not allow the temptation to be more than you can stand. When you are tempted, he will show you a way out so that you can endure."—1 Corinthians 10:13

PRIMER POWER POINT

Temptations work this way: What we say, see, read or hear moves from our minds to our hearts, and from there to our mouths, hands and feet. Maybe if we had to pay the price in advance for giving in to them, temptations wouldn't be so difficult to handle.

Wouldn't it be a great life if it could be lived without temptations? Sorry, that's not possible! We were created with body, mind and spirit which enables us to make physical, mental and spiritual decisions and choices. Temptations naturally come into play for all of us in those areas. They run the gamut from being tempted to say the wrong thing, to spend more for a bigger, better product, to eat too much of the wrong stuff, and all the way to sexual sin and even murder.

The good news is that being tempted is not a sin. It is our conscience warning us of the danger of sinning. The bad news, of course, is that we often ignore that warning and give in to temptation. It is hard to wrap your mind around it, but even Jesus was tempted in all the ways we are. Yet he did not sin. Hebrews 4:14-15 says it in so many words: "Jesus, the Son of God . . . understands our weaknesses, for he faced all of the same testing we do, yet he did not sin."

That statement is good news for all us sinners! God not only understands our problems with temptation, he's ready to help us avoid them. That help is found in the second part of verse 16: "Let us come boldly to the throne of our gracious God. There we will receive his mercy, and we will find grace to help us when we need it most." In other words, pray when you are tempted.

Being a Christian doesn't make it any easier to avoid sin. It actually makes it harder. We need to expect to fight that battle every day without any letup. Make no mistake about it, temptation is a spiritual battle with Satan. If we think we can ever win an argument with him, we're wrong. He is an extreme deceiver and a subtle devil. He causes us to rationalize bad choices by showing us the bait, which is usually pleasure, but not the hook, which is always pain.

The story of Jesus being tempted on earth by Satan is recorded in Matthew 4. As we might expect, that interaction is a great example of how we should deal with temptations. It's important to understand that temptation is a battle between our ears! And the fact is that temptations usually come at times when we are most vulnerable. Specifically, they come when we're hungry, angry, lonely, tired or depressed. At the point of Jesus' temptation after 40 days of fasting, he was hungry and obviously tired and lonely.

Satan appeals to Jesus' needs as a human being just as he does with us. And how does Jesus refute Satan? In all three aspects of his temptation, he quotes Scripture. That would be a great method to use, though an unlikely one for most of us due to our lack of detailed knowledge of the Bible. However, after the third temptation, Jesus used a method we all can and should use: He simply told Satan to "get out of here." And the devil's response was to do just that—he left! That method is simply stated in James 4:7 where it says: "Resist the devil, and he will flee from you."

Jesus resisted by audibly commanding Satan to leave. That's important because only God knows our thoughts. Satan doesn't know them, so he needs to hear us audibly refute him in Jesus' name. Of course, another effective way of dealing with the devil is to flee from him rather than waiting for him to flee from us! That simply means to stop and drop whatever is causing the temptation. James 1:14-15 has this ominous warning, "Temptation comes from our own desires, which entice us and drag us away. These desires give birth to sinful actions. And when sin is allowed to grow, it gives birth to death." In other words, let it go or let it destroy you.

We all experience temptations, but unlike Jesus, we all lose some of the battles with Satan. However, Jesus has won the war for Christians. The words of this old hymn by Charitie Lees Bancroft can be our comfort and confidence:

> Because the sinless Savior died, my sinful soul is counted free for God the just is satisfied to look on Him and pardon me.

It's that "pardon" we need to make up for those lost battles with Satan. So in the end, we win!

Jot down your impressions from this Primer. Is there something
to: **LEARN, OBEY, CONFESS or CELEBRATE?**

ON THE LIGHTER SIDE
"Always remember you are absolutely unique.
Just like everyone else."—Margaret Mead

God's Solution To Our Pollution

COMMON SENSE FROM THE BIBLE
"Everyone has sinned; we all fall short of God's glorious standard."—Romans 3:23

PRIMER POWER POINT
Sin is a human addiction, but, if we confess our sins, God says in Micah 7:19 that he will "throw them into the depths of the ocean!" Too often, we go deep-sea diving to bring back what God has "deep-sixed" rather than breathing the fresh air of his forgiveness.

Have you sinned today? How long can you go without sinning? If you have never seriously pondered those questions, the answers may shock you. But it might not shock those who know you best! In Romans 3:23, the apostle Paul made it very clear: "Everyone has sinned." He also wrote about his own struggle with sin in Romans 7:18-19: "I want to do what is right but I can't. I want to do what is good, but I don't. I don't want to do what is wrong, but I do it anyway."

Can you relate to that? Whether you're a Christian or not, we want to do what is right, don't we? We're not determined to do wrong. We don't wake up in the morning determined to offend our loved ones, break all the traffic laws on the way to work, criticize and gossip about coworkers, find fault with what's for dinner, and spend the evening ignoring or being irritated with loved ones while watching endless television shows. You can add to this list, but those are some of the kind of things Paul meant by doing wrong instead of what's good. We don't intend to do those things, but we do!

This certainly doesn't mean that we're incapable of doing good things, but it does mean our motives and tendencies almost always tilt the wrong way. It's interesting that we have to be taught to do what's right, but no one has to teach us how to do what's wrong. Lying, cheating, anger, hate, envy—they all come naturally. It all started way back at the beginning when the first humans—masterpieces of God's creation—messed up. As it did then, sin always takes us farther than we intended to stray, keeps us longer than we intended to stay, and costs more than we intended to pay. That is sin's *pollution*.

Though not often thought of this way, sin is an addiction. Like any other addiction, sin can only be overcome by recognizing a "higher power." In Alcoholics Anonymous and other organizations that help the addicted, that higher power can be just about anything. But the only real cure for sin comes from the highest power—our almighty, creator God. Our sin addiction must be surrendered to the power of his mercy and grace! That's God's *solution* to sin's *pollution!*

That solution is only available because Jesus was willing to die for the punishment we deserve. He died for those who are willing to recognize their sins, confess them, and trust him to help them live the abundant life he promised. Amazingly, through his death, we stand perfect before God! That doesn't mean we won't sin in the future, but it does mean that even those sins are covered by God's forgiveness. However, though sin is forgiven, some sins have consequences that might last a lifetime. We can't undo the wrongs of the past. But, as the "solution to our sin pollution," Jesus can offer us unconditional forgiveness for the past and a fresh start for the future.

The reality of ongoing sin should be a constant reminder of our need for God's grace. And it should remind us to make every effort to live with an attitude of gratitude for Jesus' great sacrifice. Unconfessed sin weighs us down and makes us live in fear and apprehension. Confession of sin removes that burden and frees us to face the future with hope and confidence.

The Bible tells us in Micah 7:19 that if we confess our sins, God will "throw them into the depths of the ocean!" Imagine that. Every sin has been deep-sixed by God and they now lay at the bottom of the deepest ocean. And what do we often do? We go deep-sea diving and bring them back! Once we confess, and our sins are behind us, we should never look back unless we plan to go back, because looking back keeps us from moving ahead.

So, move ahead. Get out of that dangerous, sin-infested water, take off that diving gear, take God at his word, and breathe deeply of the fresh air of his forgiveness. We can never undo what was done in the past. But God's solution to our pollution not only provides freedom and hope in this life, but a forever home—a mansion, no less—in heaven with him! What more could anyone want?

Jot down your impressions from this Primer. Is there something to: **LEARN, OBEY, CONFESS or CELEBRATE?**

ON THE LIGHTER SIDE
"A clear conscience is usually the sign of a bad memory."
—Steven Wright

Forgiving Others Is Not Optional

COMMON SENSE FROM THE BIBLE

"Make allowance for each other's faults, and forgive anyone who offends you. Remember, the Lord forgave you, so you must forgive others."—Colossians 3:13

PRIMER POWER POINT

As human beings, we can't comprehend true forgiveness because we can't forget. God does both, and until we experience his forgiveness, we can't truly forgive others. Only then, as forgiven people, can we show gratitude to God by forgiving others.

True forgiveness is literally beyond our human capacity to give or even comprehend. Anyone who is objective has to admit that while we can forgive, we literally can't forget. Only God can both forgive *and* forget. Think of God's forgiveness as his spiritual Etch A Sketch: He shakes it and our sins disappear!

Little Jimmy taught his mother a lesson on forgiveness. Expecting him to say his usual prayer after she tucked him in bed, he asked her to leave so he could say his prayers by himself. Surprised, his mom asked him if he had done something wrong. He replied that he had, but it was something he needed to talk to God about alone. He further explained that she would get upset if he told her what he had done, but if he told God, he would forgive him and forget about it!

This humorous yet poignant story is an excellent illustration of the kind of childlike faith that takes God at his word without questioning it. Who are we trying to fool anyway? God sees and hears everything we do or say. He even knows what we're thinking! Scary stuff, huh?

But only scary for those who claim to have no sin—not for anyone who confesses their sins. Though not perfect, they are forgiven!

In Matthew 18, Jesus tells a parable about a king. He had loaned money to his servants, and it is now due to be repaid. So he calls in the servant who owes him the most, and he demands payment. Upon learning the servant can't pay, the king threatens to sell all he has and throw him in prison. The servant pleads with the king, who pities him and forgives the entire debt—a huge amount!

The forgiven servant then goes to a fellow servant who owes him a small amount and demands payment. Despite pleas for a little more time, he is ruthlessly arrested and imprisoned. When the king finds out what has happened, he is furious with the ruthless servant whose large debt he had forgiven, and he has that servant thrown into prison.

Forgiveness is a two-way street. As forgiven people, we show our gratitude for God's forgiveness by forgiving others. Actually, until we understand our need for God's forgiveness, we can't genuinely forgive others, because we haven't truly experienced what it's like to be forgiven. In Colossians 3:13 Paul says this: "Make allowance for each other's faults, and forgive anyone who offends you. Remember, the Lord forgave you, so you must forgive others."

If you feel someone has hurt you, even if they don't realize that they did, the best thing you can do is to forgive them. If your relationship with that person is at all important, carrying that burden will not only hinder the relationship, it will frustrate you. Jesus said we must forgive others 70 x 7 times. In other words, an unlimited number of times, as God has forgiven us.

Forgiving someone is very liberating because it mirrors what God did for us. It frees us from anxiety and other negative feelings that take joy out of life. Of course, we should never take our sins lightly. God doesn't. To show how seriously he takes them, he gave Jesus up to a horrible death on the cross. A hymn by Stuart Townend tells this redemptive story in one short verse:

Behold the man upon a cross, my sin upon his shoulders;
Ashamed, I hear my mocking voice call out among the scoffers.
It was my sin that held him there until it was accomplished.
His dying breath has brought me life—I know that it is finished!

Incredibly, while on that cross, Jesus prayed for those who put him there. He asked God to forgive them because they didn't understand what they were doing. Though we were not physically there, it is true that our sins helped put him on that cross. Amazingly, if you were the only person who had ever sinned, he would have gone to that cross just for you. Can you believe that he would pray that same prayer for you?

Jot down your impressions from this Primer. Is there something
to: **LEARN, OBEY, CONFESS or CELEBRATE?**

_____

_____

_____

ON THE LIGHTER SIDE
A conscience makes you feel very bad right after feeling very good!

THE FEAR FACTOR

COMMON SENSE FROM THE BIBLE

"God has not given us a spirit of fear and timidity but of power, love, and self-discipline."—2 Timothy 1:7

PRIMER POWER POINT

Life can be scary. Even Jesus' disciples flipped out in fear when their boat—with Jesus in it—was caught in a storm. While he is not physically in our boat during life's storms, Jesus knows what boat we're in because his Spirit is there with us.

If you were to guess, what would you say is the most often repeated statement in the Bible? The title above provides a clue. It's "fear not" or "do not be afraid." So why is *fear* one of the emotions we deal with most often? The fact is that much about life is frightening. It's comforting to know that Jesus' own disciples and faith heroes like Moses, Joshua, David, Paul, Peter and the rest all dealt with fear. Even Jesus greatly feared his own death on the cross! In Psalm 30:6-7 (NIV), David, who God called "a man after his own heart," said: "When I felt secure, I said 'I will never be shaken' . . . but when you hid your face, I was dismayed." Can you relate to that?

Mark 4:35-41 tells us how Jesus responded to the disciples' fear when, after a long day of teaching, he was asleep in a boat. When a storm suddenly came up, the disciples feared for their lives. They woke Jesus with their screaming, "Don't you care that we're going to drown?" If the disciples flipped out in fear with Jesus in their boat, it is certainly understandable for us to fear when we're facing what appear to be oncoming life storms in our "boats." Fearful questions like: What if we lose a job? What if our business fails? What if our car needs major repairs? What if a headache is caused by a brain tumor? What if our child gets in the wrong crowd? You can add to the list.

Of course, the fear of death is very real, especially as we get older, because everyone knows we're not going to escape life alive. And in daily life, the emotions of fear we experience in times of crisis are very real. But it's important to realize that many of our fears are less certain than death, and many never happen. There's no job loss, the business doesn't fail, the car repairs aren't major, there is no brain tumor, and our child makes good friends.

We realize then that we needlessly feared potential problems. But it's important to understand that serious situations do occur, and we have to trust God to lead us through them. Interestingly, the letters in the word **FEAR** can serve as a reminder that our fears are often groundless:

False
Evidence
Appearing
Real

The premise for this acronym is expressed well in a verse from an old hymn called "God Works in a Mysterious Way" written by William Cowper in 1774: "You fearful saints, fresh courage take, the clouds you so much dread are big with mercy and shall break in blessings on your head."

Groundless or not, fear is a very real human emotion. And while Jesus is not physically in our boat, he does know what boat we're in. So when we cry out to him that life seems out of control, he understands. If Jesus understood the panic his disciples felt, we can be sure he'll understand our fears and insecurities. And it is perfectly okay to plead with him for his help. In fact, that's exactly what he wants us to do so he can help us deal with fear through faith.

It could be said that faith is fear that has said its prayers. Consider this acronym for faith: Fear Abated In Trusting Him. The only way to overcome the fear factor is through a tenacious faith and trust in God's power and promise. And as we hang on, seemingly by our fingertips at times, Jesus quietly reassures us with the same words he spoke to his disciples in Matthew 28:20, "Be sure of this: I am with you always."

Have you ever taken off in an airplane on a totally cloudy day? If so, you've probably experienced the plane breaking through the dark clouds into clear blue skies awash in bright sunshine. A feeling of exhilaration and well-being comes to those in the plane. That's the way it is when the clouds of life block our sense of God's presence.

Often, during a difficult time, we can only see the problem and have the feeling that it will never get better. Then, when the sunlight of God's love breaks through our gloom, we have that feeling of exhilaration and well-being too. God is good!

Jot down your impressions from this Primer. Is there something
to: **LEARN, OBEY, CONFESS or CELEBRATE?**

_____

_____

_____

ON THE LIGHTER SIDE
"We were born naked, wet and hungry. Then things got worse!"

FACT AND FAITH FIGHT
FEAR AND FEELINGS

COMMON SENSE FROM THE BIBLE
"God is our refuge and strength, always ready to help in times of trouble."—Psalm 46:1

PRIMER POWER POINT
If we can believe that the sun is always there, even when the clouds keep it from shining, surely we can believe that God's love is always there, even when a crisis in life keeps us from feeling it.

"God causes everything to work together for the good of those who love him." Romans 8:28 makes that promise. Along with most Christians, you may wonder sometimes how this well-known Bible verse could possibly be true. Living in a broken and dangerous world as we do, this verse should be a source of strength for Christians. However, terrorism, wars, murders and perversions of all kinds, plus our own faith-challenging fears and traumatic situations, tend to shake our trust that as the spiritual says: "He's got the whole world in his hands."

As Christians, we are not exempt from our *faith* being impacted negatively by our *feelings*, which are closely connected to the circumstances of the moment. When trauma comes, we plead with God in our *fear*. Often we can't even bring ourselves to think about God in that situation. But we must keep the eyes of our faith on God, not on our circumstances. In other words, we should glance at our circumstances and gaze on God. It is a *fact* that he will never leave us or forsake us.

Sadness, tears and mourning are facts of life, but we can't let them become a way of life. Those feelings can nearly overwhelm our faith, and the fact of God's love and concern for us can seem as empty as our aching hearts. There's an old saying that "time heals." That is true, but during that time we need to fight fear by clinging to the fact of his love, which will inspire our faith and renew our feelings. The following summarizes this process . . .

Three were walking in God's will and way: *feelings, faith and fact.*
When *fear* came up and tried to stay, *feelings* soon began to sway.
Then *faith* faltered, if truth be told, but *fact* stayed strong and bold.
Fact fought *fear* so *faith* came back, and it got *feelings* back on track.

God has the whole world in his hands. He is in total control and he always will be. He understands our doubts and fears. Because our perspective is very shortsighted, and our feelings are closely connected to the circumstances of the moment, we tend to see a hopeless end instead of endless hope. If those hopeless feelings are due to medical depression, they shouldn't be construed as a lack of faith. God created us with feelings, as is evidenced by the fact that Jesus—the strongest person in history—wept when his friend Lazarus died, and he saw how Lazarus's sisters were grieving his death.

Obviously, we have all been created with different personalities and emotional makeup. We express our feelings in different ways, and tears come from different causes and for different reasons. They can come from joy, fear, love, frustration, anger, loss, sadness, regret and other emotions. If we're really objective, we would have to admit that our emotions play a huge role in our daily lives. How we first respond to any situation is usually emotional. Depending on the circumstances, we might be glad or sad, upbeat or depressed, grateful or resentful, and so on.

Having been created in his image, it shouldn't surprise us that God experiences emotions or feelings too. The Bible records his emotional responses to the actions of people. What we do or don't do either gives him pleasure or it grieves him. While God is sinless, his responses are similar to those of earthly fathers to the actions of their children. Actually, one of his names is *Abba,* which means "Father." Some say it can mean "Daddy." As his children, thinking of God as our Heavenly Father or Daddy brings a whole new emotional dimension to our relationship with him, doesn't it?

The fact is he loves us as his children, and his love extends far beyond our greatest pleasure and deepest pain. That love will bring us to our ultimate destiny—living with Jesus in the new heaven and earth. In that eternal context, the fact is that all things do work together for the good for all who love God! Though we often can't understand it, we must hang on to that fact regardless of our feelings and circumstances. He's in those circumstances with us; he loves us, and *nothing* can separate us from his love. With Jesus on our side, fact and faith defeat fear and feelings!

Jot down your impressions from this Primer. Is there something
to: **LEARN, OBEY, CONFESS or CELEBRATE?**

ON THE LIGHTER SIDE
If you're feeling down and out, just lift up
your head and shout: I'm down and out!

PRAYER IS POWER

COMMON SENSE FROM THE BIBLE

"Don't worry about anything; instead, pray about everything. Tell God what you need, and thank him for all he has done."—Philippians 4:6

PRIMER POWER POINT

"Don't worry, pray instead." Simple to say but not so simple to practice. In tough times, it's easier to worry than to pray. In good times, we're not worried, so we don't pray. And if specific prayers aren't answered the way we think they should be, we doubt prayer's power.

There may not be a simpler statement in the Bible about the *context* and the *content* of prayer than the verse on the preceding page. The *context* is an absence of worry, and the *content* is everything. Simple enough, right? Well, not so simple, but it is true! Let's face it, our problem with prayer boils down to the fact that when we are in difficult circumstances, we don't feel like praying. And when things are going well, prayer often lands on the back burner. Then, if we do pray specifically for something, and God doesn't answer when and how we think he should, we doubt prayer's power. So why pray?

If we believe that the source of life itself is our creator God, and that he sustains us in our lives, prayer is first of all a recognition of our dependence on him. But, as independent humans, we like to think we can go it on our own—until those inevitable troubles come. Then, our confidence quickly melts away, and we feel weak and helpless. And, if we pray, it is with the desperation of a child who tearfully pleads with parents to stop a nurse from giving them a shot. Even Jesus tearfully agonized in prayer, asking that he would not have to be crucified. Of course, the parents persist because they know the child needs that shot.

Jesus persisted because he knew we, as his children, needed his sacrifice for our salvation.

Besides our independent natures, there are other reasons why most Christians struggle to have a meaningful prayer life. An important one is a lack of knowledge of how to pray. It is not unusual for mature Christians to confess that they really don't know how to pray. (Don't be put off by "mature" because most of us aren't!) It's very helpful to have a structure to guide our prayer content. A popular one is called the **ACTS** method, the content of which might look like this:

> **A**doration: Praise God for who he is, that he is in control of all, that he knows what's best (add other items of praise/adoration).
> **C**onfession: Confess that you aren't worthy of his love, that you have failed to love the way you should (add other confessions).
> **T**hanksgiving: Thank God for his patience, for loved ones, for health, strength, jobs, homes and country (add other thanks).
> **S**upplication: Ask God to meet your special needs and the needs of friends and loved ones, country and leaders (add other requests).

The ACTS prayer format can be used for prayers of any length. Here's a very simple ACTS prayer: *Dear God, I love you* (adoration). *I know I'm not worthy of your love* (confession). *Thank you for our family* (thanksgiving). *Please keep us all in your will and way* (supplication). *For Jesus' sake, Amen.*

Paul tells us to "never stop praying" in 1 Thessalonians 5:17-18. That sounds impossible until you realize that prayer doesn't have to be a structured, formalized activity. Rather, it means that we live with a prayerful awareness, in which our thoughts and concerns are actually prayers. And, when we think of an item of thanks or need, we can shoot up those quick "arrow" prayers. In times of crisis, a two-word prayer may be all we can utter: *Why? Help!* But don't forget a third word when God answers: *Thanks!*

It may often seem that our prayers are bouncing off the ceilings of heaven. If you could be sure this wasn't happening, would you make a greater commitment to pray? Maybe this will help: God hears and answers all our prayers in one of four ways:

1. If the *request* is not right, he says "No!"
2. If *you* are not right, he says "Grow!"
3. If the *time* is not right, he says "Slow!"
4. When *everything's* right, he says "Go!"

We need to remember that prayer doesn't get us around trouble, it gets us through it. Prayer doesn't make God do what we want—it helps us do what God wants! Could it be that if prayer was more of a priority, our times of crisis would be less life-wrenching? We can be sure God is always available to hear and answer us. And, though we may not always see or understand how he is working for our good, we can be very sure that he will honor our commitment to pray.

Jot down your impressions from this Primer. Is there something
to: **LEARN, OBEY, CONFESS or CELEBRATE?**

ON THE LIGHTER SIDE
We should not permit prayer to be taken out of the schools; that's
the only way most of us got through."—Sam Levenson

CHURCH: GO OR NO?

COMMON SENSE FROM THE BIBLE

"I was glad when they said to me, 'Let us go to the house of the Lord.'"—Psalm 122:1

PRIMER POWER POINT

Isn't it a bit puzzling that people will say they believe in God, but they don't need to go to church? They're really saying they can go it alone in the spiritual dimension of their lives—the one area where we need the most help, especially God's help!

Glad to go church? Are you kidding? Let's get real. Going to church isn't something we always desire to do. However, God created us as multidimensional creatures, and our spiritual dimension is a God-shaped piece in our lives that only he can fill. If that piece is missing, it's like missing the last piece of a puzzle—unsatisfying and incomplete. It started with Adam and Eve when they took a bite of that apple. They knew they had disobeyed God, so they hid and didn't want to hear from him. And people have been hiding and trying to avoid him ever since!

There are two main reasons to go to church. First, to be obedient to God's call to build a relationship with him and to worship him. If you've traveled in the parts of the world where early civilization existed, you have probably seen the remnants of churches, altars and other relics—all of which document the human recognition of the need to worship. When the apostle Paul traveled to Athens, the world center of religion in that day, he found an altar to the "unknown god" among altars to many gods. As Paul pointed out to the "wise" Athenians, the God who was unknown to them was the only true God—the one they should be worshiping. Only he could fill that missing God-shaped puzzle piece in their lives.

A second reason to go to church is to build relationships with others. Do your friends encourage you in that all-important spiritual dimension of your life? If not, you may need a change. People with addictions know that if they return to their old friends after treatment, there's an almost 100% chance of falling back into their old habits. What better place to find new friends than in church?

Isn't it a bit puzzling that people say they believe in God but they don't need to go to church? They're really saying they can go it alone in the spiritual dimension of their lives—the one area we all need the most help. Some say they don't go to church because there are a lot of hypocrites there. Probably true, but there's always room for one more!

People join special interest groups to learn more about that interest. Without a second thought, they are willing to schedule the time required. Meeting together keeps the interest level up. Why is church any different? Someone once asked theologian Dwight Moody why they should join a church. Without saying a word, Moody pulled a flaming coal away from the main fire in the hearth. Within minutes, the flame died and the coal was dead. Try this at a campfire sometime, but in the meantime, think about the power (flame) you're missing in your life if you're *not* living close to God (fire) and in positive relationships with others (coals).

If you want to keep your flame burning, find a church that applies God's Word to every aspect of living. His Word must guide our habits, hearts and home. Life is tough without the support of family and it's no different in God's family. We need to encourage each other and meet each other's needs. Going to church will help keep your flame burning!

If church is still a "no go" and you need more reasons *not* to go—or maybe why you *should* go—you might consider these:

- Because I'm poor . . . there's no admission charge!
- Because I'm rich . . . the church can help cure that!
- Because it's hot . . . so is the beach or golf course!
- Because it's raining . . . you go everywhere else in the rain!
- Because the church wants money . . . so does the grocer!
- Because I'll have time later . . . you might not have another day!

If you decide to go to church, you won't be alone and you'll probably live longer. Statistics show there are more people in churches every Sunday in the U.S. than there are at all the high school, college and pro football stadiums on any weekend. And research has found that churchgoers live longer due to less stress in their lives. If you don't go to CH_ _CH, U R missing an important way to show gratitude for God's gifts to U and his love for U!

_____

Jot down your impressions from this Primer. Is there something
to: **LEARN, OBEY, CONFESS or CELEBRATE?**

_____

_____

_____

ON THE LIGHTER SIDE
"Atheism is a non-prophet organization."—George Carlin

HEAVEN:
THE "NO MORE" PLACE

COMMON SENSE FROM THE BIBLE
"No eye has seen, no ear has heard, and no mind has imagined what God has prepared for those who love him."—1 Corinthians 2:9

PRIMER POWER POINT
Almost everyone is sure that the world will come to an end at some point. But what many are not sure of is where they will go when their lives come to an end. For Christians, real life begins in God's new heaven and earth when the world ends or their lives ends. For them the best is yet to come!

Healthy diets may be beneficial for most but not so from one man's viewpoint. His wife was extremely insistent that he should eat right and exercise regularly. As a result, he had lived ten years beyond his life expectancy when they were both killed in an accident. When they arrived at the pearly gates in heaven, they were assigned a room in a massive mansion. They were awestruck by their luxurious suite and amazed by the panoramic view from their windows and deck.

But the biggest surprise came at dinner time when they went to the enormous dining room. There they found tables overflowing with all the food the husband had so dearly desired during life before the accident. He looked at his wife, and with a touch of heavenly sarcasm said, "If it wasn't for your insistence on healthy living, we could have been here ten years ago!"

While this story may stretch credibility, 1 Corinthians 2:9 well describes the beauty of heaven: "No eye has seen, no ear has heard, and no mind has imagined what God has prepared for those who love him." To get some feeling for that, think about a mountain vista with snow-capped mountains, blue skies, green forests and gurgling streams. That is something many of us have experienced or have at least seen in a painting. Then think about heaven. Its beauty is more than anyone has ever seen or can even imagine!

Some among us have had what are often called "near-death" experiences, maybe better called "in heaven" experiences. The one commonality in all of their stories is the indescribable beauty of heaven. But heaven is much more than beauty because it is "the place of no more"—no more sickness, no more pain, no more heartbreak, no more disability, no more crying, no more bullying, and the list of "no more" goes on and on. That seems quite improbable to us inhabitants of a fallen world where all of those things are daily happenings. A place of "no more" seems to be an impossible dream. But it's much more than a dream—it's our loving creator God's promise for those who love him!

As is often the case, there is disagreement among theologians over what heaven will be like. One thing is quite clear from the Bible: there will be a new heaven and earth. In Isaiah's prophetic book, chapter 65:17 says it clearly: "Look! I am creating new heavens and a new earth, and no one will even think about the old ones anymore."

In Revelation 21:1 the apostle John wrote this about what he saw in a vision he experienced: "Then I saw a new heaven and a new earth, for the old heaven and earth had disappeared." If we can think about the natural beauty of our current heaven and earth, and then could envision it being renewed to a "no more" state of perfection, we might have just a slight conception of what heaven will be like.

So, why is an understanding of the concept of heaven important? There is a common belief that when we die—or the world ends—we'll automatically go to heaven. But the truth is that a place in heaven is only reserved for those who believe in Jesus. In Matthew 18:3 Jesus makes this very clear: "I tell you the truth, unless you turn from your sins and become like little children, you will never get into the Kingdom of Heaven." And Revelation 21:8 lists those who will not be there: cowards, unbelievers, the corrupt, murderers, the immoral, liars and more.

A teacher asked a Sunday school class who wanted to go to heaven, and all the hands went up except one. Surprised, the teacher asked the lad why he didn't raise his hand. He responded that he did want to go to heaven but not today. It was his birthday and he didn't want to miss his favorite chocolate cake!

When we are enjoying life, heaven's appeal is diminished by our toys and treasures. They may give temporary pleasure, but neither the toys nor the treasures last. At some point, our human mortality needs to be faced. No one can know when our lives will end, but we can know our destination when it happens. There are only two destinations: Heaven is all joy—hell is no joke. The choice is up to each of us!

Jot down your impressions from this Primer. Is there something
to: **LEARN, OBEY, CONFESS or CELEBRATE?**

ON THE LIGHTER SIDE
Everyone wants to live in his mansion in heaven, but many
never want to visit God's house while living on earth!

SECTION THREE

LIFE SKILL RESOURCES

Contents

FEEL FREE TO COPY ANYTHING IN
THIS SECTION OR ANY PART OF
THE BOOK FOR PERSONAL USE.

UNLOCKING YOUR LIFE SKILLS EXERCISE

Because of its importance, this segment duplicates some of the chapter by this title in Section One. Using the tools included here and committing to the following simple process for the next few months will dramatically improve the rest of your life. So let's get at it!

God created you in his image, which includes his attributes. Through practice, you can develop those attributes into life skills that enable you to get maximum benefit from the unique abilities God gave you. The apostle Paul said we should think about things that are excellent and worthy of praise, and we should practice them. With Paul's suggestions in mind, look at each of the 20 life skills on the next page and affirm that:

1. All of them would fit on Paul's list of things that are excellent and worthy of praise.

2. If you really wanted to, you could practice every one of them in your everyday life.

3. They all have an opposite word that is a negative life issue, for example: Humble—*Proud* Patient—*Impatient*

4. Each word on the list exists in you—some of the time or all of the time—in either a positive or negative way.

Assuming your agreement with these four statements, it's fair to think you'd also agree that by practicing all 20 listed life skills, they could become life skills for you. Follow the seven simple steps on the next page and you'll soon experience masterpiece living. You can do it!

SEVEN STEPS TO SUCCESSFUL LIFE SKILLS

Prior to starting this process, make copies of the Life Skill Development Tool and the Life Skill Practice Form which follow this page. Use them as indicated in steps 3 and 4 below.

Confident   Considerate   Conscientious   Content   Decisive Dependable   Disciplined   Encouraging   Faithful   Forgiving   Friendly Generous   Honest   Humble   Industrious   Kind   Loyal   Optimistic Patient   Prompt

In John 10:10, Jesus told us that his purpose was to give us a rich and satisfying life. Follow the 7 steps below to practice the 20 life skills above, and you'll soon be experiencing that kind of life. Here's how:

1. Set aside 30 minutes when you can be somewhere quiet to carefully review this life skills list without interruption.

2. Honestly ask yourself this question about every life skill on the list: *Am I normally a* (Humble) *person?*

3. Objectively rate yourself for each on this scale: *1-low*, *2-average*, *3-high*. Using a copy of the Life Skill Development Tool, jot that rating and date in the first column behind each life skill.

4. After rating and recording all 20 life skills, make a Life Skill Practice Form for each one, following the instructions on the next page. Then sort them by rating.

5. Those you rated *1-low* are your first priority to work on, so keep them with you to review and practice every day.

6. After you see progress in your *1s,* keep your *2s* with you (from #4) while continuing to work on those *1s*.

7. On a monthly basis, refer back to your original rating list and repeat steps #2-6, objectively re-rating each life skill.

LIFE SKILL DEVELOPMENT TOOL

There is room to record six monthly ratings. Undoubtedly, you (and others!) will see significant improvement much before that. But by the end of six months you will have established exciting new positive habits that you won't want to change!

Life Skill	Date	1-3	Date	1-3	Date	1-3	Date	1-3	Date	1-3	Date	1-3
Confident												
Considerate												
Conscientious												
Content												
Decisive												
Dependable												
Disciplined												
Encouraging												
Faithful												
Forgiving												
Friendly												
Generous												
Honest												
Humble												
Industrious												
Kind												
Loyal												
Optimistic												
Patient												
Prompt												

"Think about things that are excellent and worthy of praise. Keep putting into practice all that you have learned."—**Philippians 4:8-9**

LIFE SKILL PRACTICE FORMS

Make copies of this page and cut them up. Fill in the blanks and keep them with you for regular practice of Life Skills you're working on.

LIFE SKILL PRACTICE FORM SKILL _____ RATING _____ 1 = Low / 2 = Medium / 3 = High *Think about things that are excellent and worthy of praise . . . and practice them.*	**LIFE SKILL PRACTICE FORM** SKILL _____ RATING _____ 1 = Low / 2 = Medium / 3 = High *Think about things that are excellent and worthy of praise . . . and practice them.*
LIFE SKILL PRACTICE FORM SKILL _____ RATING _____ 1 = Low / 2 = Medium / 3 = High *Think about things that are excellent and worthy of praise . . . and practice them.*	**LIFE SKILL PRACTICE FORM** SKILL _____ RATING _____ 1 = Low / 2 = Medium / 3 = High *Think about things that are excellent and worthy of praise . . . and practice them.*
LIFE SKILL PRACTICE FORM SKILL _____ RATING _____ 1 = Low / 2 = Medium / 3 = High *Think about things that are excellent and worthy of praise . . . and practice them.*	**LIFE SKILL PRACTICE FORM** SKILL _____ RATING _____ 1 = Low / 2 = Medium / 3 = High *Think about things that are excellent and worthy of praise . . . and practice them.*
LIFE SKILL PRACTICE FORM SKILL _____ RATING _____ 1 = Low / 2 = Medium / 3 = High *Think about things that are excellent and worthy of praise . . . and practice them.*	**LIFE SKILL PRACTICE FORM** SKILL _____ RATING _____ 1 = Low / 2 = Medium / 3 = High *Think about things that are excellent and worthy of praise . . . and practice them.*

LIFE TRAIL INSTRUCTIONS

The *LifeTrail* tool can be used independently of this book or any other material. While the use of it is between you and God, sharing your progress—or lack of it—with an accountability partner or group greatly increases its effectiveness and benefits if used objectively. At the risk of stating the obvious, recording an assessment of your life's balance is simple.

Start by making a copy of the *LifeTrail* graphic—you can copy it as often as you wish. On a copy, place a dot in the middle of the box where you feel you are right now in your life under each of the five dimensions. Connect those dots with lines and you'll immediately see the dimensions where work is needed. Repeat this process on a regular basis, each time comparing your current assessment to your previous *LifeTrail.* Ask yourself this question about each dimension: *Have I progressed or regressed since last time?*

The attraction of a hiking trail is the natural beauty encountered along the way. The beauty causes one to hardly notice the ups and downs of the trail. But the ups and downs in real life are very noticeable. They will show up on *LifeTrail* as dimensions needing attention. Don't be discouraged. Rather, let *LifeTrail* guide your effort to get your life in balance. Because it isn't on our must-do list, the spiritual dimension usually needs the most work. *LifeTrail* can help you move the spiritual to the must-do list and hopefully to the want-to-do list!

LifeTrail Accountability Tool

This unique tool can help you level out those hills and valleys in life. However, total objectivity is critical in recording where you are in each dimension. But remember . . . perfection is all 10s, which is impossible!

A	B	C	D	E
SPIRITUAL	PHYSICAL	MENTAL	RELATIONAL	FINANCIAL
Prayer	Fitness	Attitude	Marriage	Saving
Worship	Nutrition	Habits	Family	Spending
Devotions	Recreation	Thoughts	Friends	Giving

	A	B	C	D	E
10					
9					
8					
7					
6					
5					
4					
3					
2					
1					

FOUNDATION OF FAITH

"Those who trust in the Lord will find new strength. They will soar high on wings like eagles."—Isaiah 40:31

God created us as multidimensional beings, and all the dimensions are connected. When one suffers, they all suffer, so balance between each of those dimensions is the goal. You will discover that the higher and straighter your graph line is, the more content and happier you'll be!

GOAL ACHIEVEMENT INSTRUCTIONS

In its simplest form, the process for goal setting or achievement is the same as your weekly grocery shopping list. Look at the form on the next page and follow each step indicated:

- **Goal to be Achieved:** *Buy the grocery list items*
- *LifeTrail* **Dimension:** *Physical*
- **Achieve by:** *Saturday noon*
- **Benefits of Achieving:** *Enjoyment of eating / Staying healthy*
- **Obstacles to Achieving:** *Busy schedule / Car availability*
- **Actions to Achieve:** *Set a date and time / Arrange for car*
- **Comments:** *Don't forget coupons / Avoid impulse buying*

Obviously, things that we do on a daily basis don't require a formal plan to achieve them. But even then, to avoid forgetting something important, it's wise to put a grocery list or a daily to-do list in writing. So with the example above in your mind, think about goals such as going on vacation, buying a car or getting a job. Using the Goal Achievement Tool on the next page will help you achieve those goals. Goals must be *specific*, *realistic* and *legitimate*. That tool will help you meet the specific and realistic guidelines. The *LifeTrail* graphic on the previous page will help you determine if a goal is legitimate for you.

As you refer back to *LifeTrail* now, let's say you wanted to buy a larger home. Measure that goal against each of the *LifeTrail* dimensions, and make an honest judgment by answering this question: Does that goal have a positive or negative impact on your priorities in each dimension? A larger, more expensive home might have a positive effect on the social dimension, but if you have to work more hours or borrow more money to afford it, that could have a negative impact on marriage and family relationships and/or the spiritual dimension.

The Goal Achievement Tool and *LifeTrail* can serve together as dynamic tools to help you set goals within the right priorities that lead to a balanced, truly successful life. Reaching legitimate goals is very satisfying, motivating and life-giving. That's what Solomon meant in Proverbs 13:12 when he said: "A dream fulfilled is a tree of life!"

GOAL ACHIEVEMENT TOOL

A GOAL WITHOUT A PLAN IS SIMPLY A DREAM!

Desired Goal to be Achieved _____

_____

LifeTrail Dimension _____

Start Date: _____ / _____   **Achieve by:** _____ / _____

Benefits of Achieving _____

_____

Obstacles to Achieving _____

_____

Actions to Achieve _____

_____

_____

_____

_____

Notes _____

_____

_____

LifeSkillPrimer Application Guides

The story of the pump very clearly described the importance of what was needed to successfully draw water out of the well. The pump needed to be primed, meaning water had to be put into it before water could be drawn up. Priming the pump of life is the purpose of the topical *LifeSkillPrimers* found in Section Two. Just as the pump takes pumping effort to produce water, working through the Application Guides in this section represent that effort to produce results in our lives. These guides are in the same order as the topical chapters which start on page 52. They should be reviewed before working through the guide's exercises.

Each guide includes five questions for individual consideration or small group discussion. These guides also include a section for counting your blessings. You will probably admit that counting your blessings is sadly neglected far too often. We take so much for granted, and we're so good at counting the blessings of others that we are often blind to our own.

Last but not least is the short prayer included in all the guides. Each prayer follows the ACTS format explained in the *LifeSkillPrimer* entitled "Prayer is Power." Regular use of those simple prayers will help you develop your relationship with God, as well as cultivating contentment through an attitude of gratitude for his provision and power in your life.

APPLICATION GUIDE TOPICS

This is a topical index of the Application Guides that follow in the order listed. They correspond in that order to the related *LifeSkillPrimers* in Section Two starting on page 52. Note that they are grouped by three dimensions of our human existence: physical, mental and spiritual.

MONEY: ROOT OF EVIL OR TREE OF BLESSING?
Application Guide

Read this and then reflect on/discuss the following questions:
Zig Ziglar said, "You don't pay the price for success—you enjoy the benefits. You pay the price for failure." In Luke 12:48, Jesus said: "When someone has been given much, much will be required in return."

1. Does it make sense that we pay the price for failing to give?

2. How do you determine how much is required of you?

3. Do Christians have a greater responsibility to share?

4. Can the income from using your abilities be God's gift to you?

5. Do you ever feel guilty about having money and possessions?

Reflect on/discuss this lesson's Primer Power Point:
The love of money can get us in trouble. But through acts of generosity, money becomes a tree of blessing rather than the root of evil. Then we can enjoy the fruits of our labor while guarding our hearts from growing roots in the pleasures of the world.

Life Skill Blessings Log
Count Your Blessings, Name Them One by One
If you are thankful for what you have, it will become what you want!

_____

_____

_____

PRAYER: *Dear God, you are amazingly generous. I confess that I too often give begrudgingly. Thank you for the blessings you shower on me day after day. Help me to share more willingly and to be a tree of blessing for those around me for Jesus' sake, Amen.*

STEWARDSHIP: GIVING, SAVING AND SPENDING
Application Guide

Read this and then reflect on/discuss the questions that follow:
Nothing in this world imitates God like giving does. Giving breaks the grip of greed. You'll be remembered not by what you have acquired but by what you gave away.

1. Can you relate to the rich man's attachment to his stuff?

2. Why did Jesus tell him he needed to sell all that he had?

3. How has money defined your life?

4. Is giving a priority for you or is it an afterthought?

5. Is it possible to "give eagerly" as Paul suggested below?

Reflect on/discuss this lesson's Primer Power Point:
"Whatever you give is acceptable if you give it eagerly. And give according to what you have . . . Of course, I don't mean your giving should make life easy for others and hard for yourselves."
—The apostle Paul (2 Corinthians 8:12-13)

Life Skill Blessings Log
Count Your Blessings, Name Them One by One
If you are thankful for what you have, it will become what you want!

_____

_____

_____

PRAYER: *Dear God, you are the great provider. I confess I have missed opportunities to be a provider for others. I'm thankful for how you have provided for me in abundance. Help me to become a better steward of your provision by giving to others in Jesus' name, Amen.*

WORK: THERAPY FOR BODY AND SOUL
Application Guide

Read this and then reflect on/discuss the questions that follow:
You may experience setbacks in life, but they are challenges to overcome—not excuses for giving up.

1. Do you see setbacks as challenges rather than excuses?

2. Can you be busy making a living and miss making a life?

3. How does God reward us if we work as if working for him?

4. Do you believe that the work you do is a calling from God?

5. Could a public works program be better than giving welfare?

Reflect on/discuss this lesson's Primer Power Point:
A statement at the Franklin D. Roosevelt Memorial in Washington, D.C. brilliantly defines the importance of work: "No country, however rich, can afford the waste of its human resources. Demoralization caused by vast unemployment is our greatest extravagance. Morally, it is the greatest menace to our social order."

Life Skill Blessings Log
Count Your Blessings, Name Them One by One
If you are thankful for what you have, it will become what you want!

_____

_____

_____

PRAYER: *Dear God, your work in creation is amazing! I confess that, like so many other blessings, I take my work for granted. Thank you for that work. Help me to have an attitude of gratitude in my work that allows others to see you in me for Jesus' sake, Amen.*

GOALS & PRIORITIES: DISCIPLINES
OF A SUCCESSFUL LIFE
Application Guide

Read this and then reflect on/discuss the questions that follow:
Though not wrong in themselves, it's dangerous to measure success by financial achievements, because they are actually forms of failure if priorities are wrong.

1. Are you satisfied with the priorities and balance in your life?

2. Does it motivate you to accomplish a task/to-do list?

3. Have you ever set goals in a formal way?

4. How is a dream fulfilled like "a tree of life?"

5. How are you doing in committing your plans to the Lord?

Reflect on/discuss this lesson's Primer Power Point:
Learn from these wise men. Solomon: "A dream fulfilled is a tree of life." Billy Graham: "Until a man gets his priorities in life straight, everything else is going to be out of order." Ben Franklin: "Motivation is when your dreams put on work clothes."

Life Skill Blessings Log
Count Your Blessings, Name Them One by One
If you are thankful for what you have, it will become what you want!

_____
_____
_____

PRAYER: *Dear God, you are a loving God. Forgive me for not making you a priority in life. Thank you for the promise to prosper my plans. Help me commit them to you in Jesus' name, Amen.*

INTEGRITY: A LEGACY FOR LIFE
Application Guide

Read this and then reflect on/discuss the questions that follow:
People who are faithful in their relationships and honest in their dealings are respected for their integrity. They don't have to worry about being burdened by guilt from past or present activities.

1. Why doesn't everyone do what's right and honorable?

2. How do your spiritual beliefs fit into integrity?

3. What motivates non-religious people to have integrity?

4. Are there degrees of integrity?

5. Do you act differently when no one is looking?

Reflect on/discuss this lesson's Primer Power Point:
Integrity is a by-product of practicing God's attributes created in us. It defines the person who does the right thing even when no one is watching or is in a position to know what was done. People of integrity leave a lasting legacy for everyone with whom they have contact, especially succeeding generations.

Life Skill Blessings Log
Count Your Blessings, Name Them One by One
If you are thankful for what you have, it will become what you want!

_____

_____

_____

PRAYER: *Dear God, your integrity is totally trustworthy. I confess that mine is not. Thank you for loving me anyway. Please guide me in such a way that I will leave a legacy of integrity despite my failings. For Jesus' sake, Amen.*

REWARDING RELATIONSHIPS
Application Guide

Read this and then reflect on/discuss the questions that follow:
"Don't look out only for your own interests, but take an interest in others, too."
—*Philippians 2:4*

1. When did you last smile at, greet or help a stranger?

2. How could you be more proactive in being "others-oriented"?

3. Can you forgive yourself and others for causing hurt?

4. Is it often easier to be nicer to others than to loved ones?

5. How could tomorrow be too late to treasure your loved ones?

Reflect on/discuss this lesson's Primer Power Point:
In Matthew 7:12 Jesus stated what is widely known as the Golden Rule: "Do to others whatever you would like them to do to you." Just a simple smile or kind word, especially to those in need, encourages them today and brightens their tomorrows . . . and yours!

Life Skill Blessings Log
Count Your Blessings, Name Them One by One
If you are thankful for what you have, it will become what you want!

_____

_____

_____

PRAYER: *Dear God, make me an instrument of your peace . . . grant that I may not so much seek to be consoled as to console, to be understood as to understand, to be loved as to love. Amen.*

(*From the* Peace Prayer *by St. Francis of Assisi*)

MARRIAGE & FAMILY: NO EXPERIENCE REQUIRED
Application Guide

Read this and then reflect on/discuss the following questions:
Submission to each other is a voluntary decision that is one of the important ingredients in a strong relationship. Jesus' submission to the cross for those he loved is the example of what we should be willing to do for those we love.

1. Why is it so difficult to be submissive to another person?

2. What are other ingredients in a strong marriage relationship?

3. Prayer is one of those ingredients. Do you pray together?

4. What special things can be done to keep your marriage strong?

5. Are you aware that you are training your children to be loving partners as well as parents?

Reflect on/discuss this lesson's Primer Power Point:
Stranger than fiction: What lifelong commitment would anyone in their right mind ever make without learning what is required by that commitment or being trained to perform all the requirements of it? It's called getting married and raising a family!

Life Skill Blessings Log
Count Your Blessings, Name Them One by One
If you are thankful for what you have, it will become what you want!

_____

_____

_____

PRAYER: *Dear God, your plan for our marriages and families is a great one. Please forgive us for messing it up so badly. Thank you for recreating us in Jesus, making it possible to do the good things you planned for us. Help me to live as your masterpiece in your world for your glory, in Jesus' name, Amen.*

THE POWER OF A POSITIVE ATTITUDE
Application Guide

Read this and then reflect on/discuss the questions that follow:
"A positive attitude won't enable you to do everything, but it will help you do everything better than a negative attitude will." —Zig Ziglar

1. How can this quote from Ziglar be applied to life?

2. Why would God want you to have a positive attitude?

3. What is your biggest obstacle to being more positive?

4. Do others see you as more positive than loved ones do?

5. Is it possible to act your way into feeling more positive?

Reflect on/discuss this lesson's Primer Power Point:
The mind can be used for both good and evil. As humans, we tend toward evil. A powerful weapon for combatting that tendency is a positive attitude, which is life-healing, while a negative attitude is life-hardening. Both are extremely contagious!

Life Skill Blessings Log
Count Your Blessings, Name Them One by One
If you are thankful for what you have, it will become what you want!

_____

_____

_____

PRAYER: *Dear God, you are the original positive thinker! I confess the negative thoughts and attitudes I have far too often. I'm thankful for examples in the Bible of those who have shown how powerful a positive attitude can be in all of life. Help me to be renewed in the attitude of my mind for Jesus' sake, Amen.*

THE PROMISE OF PERSEVERANCE
Application Guide

Read this and then reflect on/discuss the questions that follow:
Abraham Lincoln said, "My great concern is not whether you have failed, but whether you are content with your failure."

1. What did Lincoln imply would keep us from failing?

2. How have you persevered in times of drudgery or frustration?

3. Share a time when you had to exert unusual perseverance.

4. Why didn't the master give each servant the same amount?

5. How are you using your abilities rather than burying them?

Reflect on/discuss this lesson's Primer Power Point:
There's a close connection between perseverance and our abilities. Perseverance is a life skill which unlocks and enables the abilities God has entrusted to each of us. We become what he intended us to be through persevering in using those abilities.

Life Skill Blessings Log
Count Your Blessings, Name Them One by One
If you are thankful for what you have, it will become what you want!

_____
_____
_____

PRAYER: *Dear God, you are a good and gracious God. I confess that I don't depend enough on your strength. Thank you for the promise of perseverance. Help me claim that promise to your glory, in the name of Jesus, who persevered through so much for me, Amen.*

CONTENTMENT: THE ATTITUDE OF GRATITUDE
Application Guide

Read this and then reflect on/discuss the questions that follow:
Ben Franklin posed these questions and answers: "Who is wise? He who learns from everyone. Who is powerful? He who governs his passions. Who is rich? He who is content. Who is that? Nobody!"

1. What is Franklin implying by these questions and answers?

2. Can we learn how to be content in any situation like Paul did?

3. How is an "attitude of gratitude" an antidote to coveting?

4. Why doesn't getting what you want result in contentment?

5. What's the difference between contentment and happiness?

Reflect on/discuss this lesson's Primer Power Point:
Our contentment should never depend on our comfortable circumstances, material possessions or freedom from pain or sorrow. Rather, it must come from gratitude to God for our relationship with him, trusting him for what we need—not what we want.

Life Skill Blessings Log
Count Your Blessings, Name Them One by One
If you are thankful for what you have, it will become what you want!

_____

_____

_____

PRAYER: *Dear God, you are a generous God. Forgive me for my discontent in spite of having so much. Thank you for all that you have given and forgiven. Please help me develop an attitude of gratitude and be an example of your love for Jesus' sake, Amen.*

HABITS: YOU ARE WHAT THEY ARE
Application Guide

Read this and then reflect on/discuss the questions that follow:
"It may be the devil or it may be the Lord, but you're gonna have to serve somebody."   —Bob Dylan

1. Can you relate to Dylan's lyrics about who you serve?

2. How does who you serve affect your habits?

3. What does it mean to serve someone or something?

4. Does Paul's struggle with sin help you understand your own?

5. How are good habits related to an athlete's mechanics?

Reflect on/discuss this lesson's Primer Power Point:
Edmund Burke said that "those who don't know history are destined to repeat it." Though that was said in a national context, there is great wisdom in applying that statement to individual human life as it relates to learning from our habits—good or bad.

Life Skill Blessings Log
Count Your Blessings, Name Them One by One
If you are thankful for what you have, it will become what you want!

_____

_____

_____

PRAYER: *Dear God, you are truly gracious and patient. I am not worthy of serving you. Thank you for the simple message that I have to make a choice of serving you or the devil. I want to serve you, weak as I am, for Jesus' sake, Amen.*

CHOICES: PLANTING YOUR HARVEST
Application Guide

Read this and then reflect on/discuss the following questions:
"Don't be misled . . . You will always harvest what you plant."

—Galatians 6:7

1. Why doesn't God keep us from making poor choices?

2. Are you aware of the need to please God with your choices?

3. Have you made bad choices when instinct warns you not to?

4. Would it help to run potential choices past a trusted friend?

5. How can we be sure we're making the right choice?

Reflect on/discuss this lesson's Primer Power Point:
Starting with the first family, history is filled with ruined lives due to bad choices. Watch the news and you'll see lives of politicians and celebrities implode in living color. Unbelievable? Be careful—none of us are immune to making bad choices!

Life Skill Blessings Log
Count Your Blessings, Name Them One by One
If you are thankful for what you have, it will become what you want!

PRAYER: *Dear God, you chose to create a perfect world. I confess the foolish choices I have made in the past. Thank you for your forgiveness of them. Please impress on me the choices I need to make in the future by pondering what you desire for me for Jesus' sake, Amen.*

PRIDE & JEALOUSY: A DEADLY COMBINATION
Application Guide

Read this and then reflect on/discuss the questions that follow:
Practicing humility will have a very positive effect on life balance, especially in the spiritual and relational dimensions. We should all choose to "die" to selfish pride. That would be a "death" we could benefit from while we're still living.

1. Can you practice humility?

2. Think of a time you've been humbled. How did you feel?

3. What is the difference between pride and jealousy?

4. Is it okay to be proud when you succeed at something?

5. How can we "die" to selfish pride?

Reflect on/discuss this lesson's Primer Power Point:
Like any other human failing, pride is not an unforgivable sin. It is simply more evidence of our need for God's forgiveness, which he promises if we repent. Of course, God doesn't honor our sin, but he does honor our repentance.

Life Skill Blessings Log
Count Your Blessings, Name Them One by One
If you are thankful for what you have, it will become what you want!

_____

_____

_____

PRAYER: *Dear God, your humility is beyond my understanding. I confess the pride and jealousy that I deal with every day. Thank you for the assurance that you honor my repentance, as weak as that may be. Please help me honor Jesus who went to the cross to pay the price of my pride. In his name, Amen.*

TEMPTATION: A COMMON AFFLICTION
Application Guide

Read this and then reflect on/discuss the questions that follow:
The normal desires created in us by God can become powerful tools of the devil. He appeals to our instincts that satisfy those desires, and he tempts us to selfishly abuse them.

1. How do temptations distort valid desires?

2. Does it help you to know that Jesus experienced temptations?

3. Have you ever refuted the devil audibly or run from him?

4. How is self-control helpful in dealing with temptations?

5. What kind of price do we pay for losing a temptation battle?

Reflect on/discuss this lesson's Primer Power Point:
Temptations work this way: What we say, see, read or hear moves from our minds into our hearts, and from there to our mouths, hands and feet. Maybe if we had to pay the price in advance for giving in to them, temptations wouldn't be so difficult to handle.

Life Skill Blessings Log
Count Your Blessings, Name Them One by One
If you are thankful for what you have, it will become what you want!

_____

_____

_____

PRAYER: *Dear God, you are a God worthy of our service. I confess my willingness to serve the devil rather than you. Thank you for understanding my temptations. Please help me refute Satan and serve you in my thoughts, words and deeds for Jesus' sake, Amen.*

GOD'S SOLUTION TO OUR POLLUTION
Application Guide

Read this and then reflect on/discuss the questions that follow:
The reality is that we sin in thought, word and deed. And God knows every thought, hears every word, and sees every deed. If we are to live in that reality, we need to answer these questions:

1. What thoughts should I change?

2. What words shouldn't I say?

3. What activities should I avoid?

4. What attitudes should I adjust?

5. What motives should I correct?

Reflect on/discuss this lesson's Primer Power Point:
Sin is a human addiction, but, if we confess our sins, God says in Micah 7:19 that he will "throw them into the depths of the ocean." Too often, we go deep-sea diving to bring back what God has deep-sixed rather than breathing the fresh air of his forgiveness.

Life Skill Blessings Log
Count Your Blessings, Name Them One by One
If you are thankful for what you have, it will become what you want!

_____

_____

_____

PRAYER: *Dear God, despite knowing my thoughts, words and deeds, you are still willing to forgive me. I confess my unworthiness. Thank you for your amazing grace. Please help me live in a way that shows my gratitude and brings glory to Jesus for his sake, Amen.*

FORGIVING OTHERS IS NOT OPTIONAL
Application Guide

Read this and then reflect on/discuss the questions that follow:
If you have been offended, and the one who offended you doesn't even realize it, the best thing you can do is forgive them. If you don't, that relationship can never be the same. That's why Jesus said that we must forgive others 70x7 times!

1. Do you believe God can forget your most serious sin?

2. Why can't we forget our sins or those of others?

3. What excuses do we make for not forgiving others?

4. How can you forgive someone who isn't sorry?

5. What did Jesus mean that we need to forgive 70x7?

Reflect on/discuss this lesson's Primer Power Point:
As human beings, we can't comprehend true forgiveness because we can't forget. God does both, and until we experience his forgiveness, we can't truly forgive others. Only then, as forgiven people, we show our gratitude to God by forgiving others.

Life Skill Blessings Log
Count Your Blessings. Name Them One by One
If you are thankful for what you have, it will become what you want!

_____

_____

_____

PRAYER: *Dear God, your forgiveness is amazing and beyond my comprehension. I confess my unworthiness. I'm so thankful that Jesus was willing to die and make me worthy in your sight. Help me to show my gratitude by forgiving others for Jesus' sake, Amen.*

THE FEAR FACTOR
Application Guide

Read this and then reflect on/discuss the following questions:
"When I felt secure, I said I will never be shaken. But when you hid your face, I was dismayed." —King David, Psalm 30:6 (NIV)

1. What makes you feel secure?

2. What "shakes" you or causes you dismay?

3. What does it mean that God "hides his face?"

4. Do you feel like praying when you're fearful?

5. Is trusting God difficult in times of stress and fear?

Reflect on/discuss this lesson's Primer Power Point:
Life can be scary. Even Jesus' disciples flipped out in fear when their boat— with Jesus in it—was caught in a storm. While he is not physically in our boat during life's storms, Jesus knows what boat we're in because his Spirit is there with us.

Life Skill Blessings Log
Count Your Blessings, Name Them One by One
If you are thankful for what you have, it will become what you want!

_____
_____
_____

PRAYER: *Dear God, you are a God with a love that casts out fear. Too often, my fear blocks my ability to trust your love. Thank you for your promise to always be with me. Please help me face my challenges with faith rather than fear for Jesus' sake, Amen.*

FACT & FAITH FIGHT FEAR & FEELINGS
Application Guide

Read this and then reflect on/discuss the questions that follow:
You don't feel your way into a new way of acting, you act your way into a new way of feeling.

1. Are you able to put on a good front when feeling down?

2. Have you experienced **F**alse **E**vidence **A**ppearing **R**eal?

3. Does considering God a loving parent help you relate to him?

4. Can you trust God's presence in times of stress and trouble?

5. Recall a time when life's clouds gave way to God's love.

Reflect on/discuss this lesson's Primer Power Point:
If we can believe that the sun is always there, even when the clouds keep it from shining, surely we can believe that God's love is always there, even when a crisis in life keeps us from feeling it!

Life Skill Blessings Log
Count Your Blessings, Name Them One by One
If you are thankful for what you have, it will become what you want!

_____

_____

_____

PRAYER: *Dear God, your control over all the world is awesome! I confess that I don't live with that confidence. Thank you for always being there. Strengthen my faith by that fact for Jesus' sake, Amen.*

PRAYER IS POWER
Application Guide

Read this and then reflect on/discuss the following questions:
How we pray changes how we live. How we live changes how we pray. Pray about everything, don't worry about anything.

1. How does prayer change how we live?

2. Is there a difference between being concerned and worrying?

3. Have you ever experienced answers to prayer?

4. What does it mean to pray about everything?

5. Why do you—or should you—keep a prayer list?

Reflect on/discuss this lesson's Primer Power Point:
"Don't worry, pray instead." Simple to say, but not so simple to practice. In tough times, it's easier to worry than to pray. In good times, we're not worried, so we don't pray. And if specific prayers aren't answered how we think they should be, we doubt prayer's power.

Life Skill Blessings Log
Count Your Blessings, Name Them One by One
If you are thankful for what you have, it will become what you want!

_____

_____

_____

PRAYER: *Dear God, you are an awesome God who gave us the power of prayer. I know I don't depend on that power enough. Thank you for your promise to hear and answer all my prayers. Please help me to be more faithful in my prayer life for Jesus' sake, Amen.*

CHURCH: GO OR NO?
Application Guide

Read this and then reflect on/discuss the questions that follow:
"Going to church doesn't make you a Christian any more than going to a garage makes you an automobile." —Billy Sunday

1. What does it mean that we have a spiritual dimension?

2. If you go to church on occasion, why?

3. If you don't go to church at all, why not?

4. Does it influence you if your friends don't go to church?

5. How does church attendance show gratitude to God?

Reflect on/discuss this lesson's Primer Power Point:
Isn't it a bit puzzling that people will say they believe in God, but they don't need to go to church? They're really saying they can go it alone in the spiritual dimension of their lives—the one area where we need the most help, especially God's help!

Life Skill Blessings Log
Count Your Blessings, Name Them One by One
If you are thankful for what you have, it will become what you want!

_____

_____

_____

PRAYER: *Dear God, it's amazing that you want our praise and worship. I confess that is not something I desire to do most of the time. Thank you for reminding me today of your desire. Please help me to want to seek your will for my life for Jesus' sake, Amen.*

HEAVEN: THE "NO MORE" PLACE
Application Guide

Read this and then reflect on/discuss the following questions:
The late Tony Snow, who served as Press Secretary under President George W. Bush, made this statement after learning that he had terminal cancer: "God doesn't promise us life for tomorrow but he does promise us eternal life when this life ends."

1. Do you think about where you will go at the end of your life?

2. What are the requirements for going to heaven?

3. Are you sure you will go to heaven? Why or why not?

4. Who will not go to heaven?

5. Can someone be so bad that they can't go to heaven?

Reflect on/discuss this lesson's Primer Power Point:
Almost everyone is sure that the world will come to an end at some point. But what many are not sure of is where they will go when their lives come to an end. For Christians, real life begins in God's new heaven and earth when the world ends or their lives end. For believers the best is yet to come!

Life Skill Blessings Log
Count Your Blessings, Name Them One by One
If you are thankful for what you have, it will become what you want!

_____
_____
_____

PRAYER: *Dear God, I praise you for wanting me to live with you in eternity. I confess my lack of gratitude for that promise. Help me to live with confidence that the best is yet to come. For Jesus' sake, Amen.*

These are *PocketPowerPrimers*...copy them often and cut them up to carry with you for regular review to keep your "pump of life primed." You can also share them with others for their encouragement such as leaving one with your tip in restaurants.

WHY YOU? WHY HERE? WHY NOW? NOW WHAT?
"I know the plans I have for you . . . plans for good . . . to give you a future and a hope." **Common Sense from the Bible**—*Jer. 29:11*

Have you ever wondered who you are and why you're here at this time in history? In other words, have you ever questioned the purpose of your life? It's thought that Mark Twain said "The two most important days in your life are the day you are born and the day you find out why." Finding out why refers to answering questions which will help you discover who you are and why you exist. The verse above says that God has plans for us. And Ephesians 2:10 says: "We are God's masterpiece. He has created us anew in Christ Jesus so we can do the good things he planned for us long ago." It certainly doesn't sound like God wants us to aimlessly drift through life, does it? His book, the Bible, overflows with common sense answers to life's questions!

WHAT IS TRUE SUCCESS?
"What do you benefit if you gain the whole world but lose your own soul?" **Common Sense from the Bible**—*Matt. 16:26*

What is true success? We are so blessed to live in a country which was founded on biblical principles such as justice, integrity, freedom, trust, diligence and more. Practicing those principles has empowered a free enterprise system that rewards individual effort using God-given abilities. The resulting financial achievements can contribute to true success. However, they are only a form of failure if our priorities are wrong. In Luke 12:48 Jesus said, "When someone has been given much, much will be required in return." True success results from using personal achievement to serve others. Read the verse at the top again and think about this: what you believe is much more important than any financial goals you might achieve!

UNLOCKING YOUR SUCCESSFUL LIFE SKILLS
"Think about things that are excellent and worthy of praise." **Common Sense from the Bible**—*Phil. 4:8*

God created us in his own image! What that means has been the topic of discussion for centuries with no definitive answers. But his image in us most certainly includes the qualities of his character—his attributes. No doubt, Paul was referring to them in the verse above. He further identified some of those attributes in Galatians 5:22-23 as patience, kindness, gentleness, faithfulness and self-control. There are many other "excellent and worthy of praise" attributes, but the point is that God planted them in us as part of his image. By practicing those attributes as Paul prescribes, they will become life skills that empower us to maximize our God-given abilities, resulting in a greater level of success in every dimension of our lives!

These are *PocketPowerPrimers*...copy them often and cut them up to carry with you for regular review to keep your "pump of life primed." You can also share them with others for their encouragement such as leaving one with your tip in restaurants.

MONEY: ROOT OF EVIL OR TREE OF BLESSING?

"Give freely and become more wealthy . . . the generous will prosper; those who refresh others will themselves be refreshed." **Common Sense from the Bible—*Prov. 11:24-25***

Amazing, isn't it, that the topic of money found its way into so many of Jesus' parables and conversations? In fact, money is the most oft-mentioned topic in the Bible. Why? Because money matters a lot! But money and possessions carry with them a huge responsibility for Christians. When we aren't content with what we have, money can easily become the "root of evil" Jesus warned about. However, if we honor God with our wealth—and most of us are wealthy by world standards—through acts of generosity and sharing, money can be a tree of blessing. Then, as the generous prosper and give freely, they not only refresh others, but they themselves will be refreshed!

STEWARDSHIP: GIVING, SAVING & SPENDING

"God loves a person who gives cheerfully." **Common Sense from the Bible—*2 Cor. 9:7***

Hoping to develop character in his son, a father gave the boy a quarter and a dime. One coin should go to Sunday school and spend the other. Eagerly, the father later asked the son which coin he gave. Very calmly, the son said that he knew God loved a cheerful giver, so he gave the dime, which he could give much more cheerfully than the quarter! Obviously, the son had given thought to what he should do. That's a good first step, because if giving is an afterthought, it will soon be a lost thought. There is never an easy time to give. We need to remember that all we have—our time, talents and treasure—is given to us by God. His gifts have probably raised our standard of living, so we can be sure he wants us to raise our standard of giving!

WORK: THERAPY FOR BODY AND SOUL

"There is nothing better than to enjoy food and drink and to find satisfaction in work . . . these pleasures are from the hand of God." **Common Sense from the Bible—*Eccles. 2:24***

Former U.S. president, Franklin Roosevelt, made this statement: "No country, however rich, can afford the waste of its human resources. Demoralization caused by vast unemployment is our greatest extravagance. Morally, it is the greatest menace to our social order." Our legitimate occupations are callings from God. Using our unique abilities produces income that gives us purpose and fulfillment in life, and supports the common good of society. In Ephesians 6:7-8, Paul talks about the importance of our attitude toward work. He encourages us to work enthusiastically as if we were working for the Lord who "will reward each one of us for the good we do."

These are *PocketPowerPrimers*...copy them often and cut them up to carry with you for regular review to keep your "pump of life primed." You can also share them with others for their encouragement such as leaving one with your tip in restaurants.

GOALS AND PRIORITIES: KEYS TO SUCCESSFUL LIVING
"Good planning and hard work lead to prosperity,
but hasty shortcuts lead to poverty."
Common Sense from the Bible—*Prov. 21:5*

Walt Disney said, "Our dreams can come true if we have the courage to pursue them." Billy Graham said: "Until a man gets his priorities in order, everything else is going to be out of order." These wise men are saying that a dream is a goal guided by the right priorities. Setting goals is nothing more than making plans, which, if made within each dimension of life's priorities, will provide balance, direction and motivation for life. The wise Ben Franklin said: "Motivation is when your dreams put on work clothes." Reaching one's goals can be exciting and life-giving! That's what a fourth wise man, Solomon, meant in Proverbs 13:12: "A dream fulfilled is a tree of life!

INTEGRITY: A LEGACY FOR LIFE
"People with integrity walk safely ... those who follow crooked paths
will slip and fall." **Common Sense from the Bible**—*Prov. 10:9*

All humanity struggles with integrity. It defines the person who does the right thing even when no one would know the difference. It'd be nice if we were all born with integrity, but babies aren't around long before they prove that to be a fantasy. They quickly show the long reach of Adam and Eve's legacy of bad choices, providing proof that integrity doesn't come as standard equipment on humans! Integrity is the byproduct of practicing God's attributes which he created in us. It is one of the key traits of all truly successful people. Integrity must be your guide if you want to "walk safely" through life with all its obstacles and challenges. That is the only way to leave a legacy of integrity for succeeding generations.

REWARDING RELATIONSHIPS
Jesus said, "Do to others whatever you would like them to
do to you." **Common Sense from the Bible**—*Matt. 7:12*

Paying it forward is a popular thing to do. That is essentially what Jesus is saying in the verse above, widely known as the Golden Rule. Another way of saying that is: "Treat others right and they'll treat you right." Every day of life is full of opportunities to encourage others in some way. We only need to be sensitive to them and have a willing spirit to respond. Just a smile, a friendly greeting, or even paying a few dollars for groceries for someone goes a long way to encouraging others today and brightening their tomorrows. Simple stuff like that will contribute to positive relationships and contentment in life. Being considerate of others, especially those who may be in need, will bless their lives—and yours!

These are *PocketPowerPrimers*...copy them often and cut them up to carry with you for regular review to keep your "pump of life primed." You can also share them with others for their encouragement such as leaving one with your tip in restaurants.

THE POWER OF A POSITIVE ATTITUDE

Be made new in the attitude of your minds and . . . put on the new self. **Common Sense from the Bible —*Eph. 4:23-24* (NIV)**

In the early 1940s, Johnny Mercer made a song popular which repeated these lyrics: "You got to accentuate the positive, eliminate the negative." While our world churns around us, as it has from the beginning of time, accentuating the positive can be a real challenge. Add the chaotic world situation to our personal or family challenges, and we can easily succumb to negativity. But we can't let the challenges of life keep us down. The attitude of your mind can be positive, which is life-healing, or negative, which is life-hardening. Both are extremely contagious. Zig Ziglar said: "A positive attitude won't enable you to do everything, but it will help you do everything better than a negative attitude will!"

THE PROMISE OF PERSEVERANCE

"Whoever pursues righteousness and love, finds life, prosperity and honor." **Common Sense from the Bible—*Prov. 21:21* (NIV)**

To persevere means to "keep on keeping on" through whatever obstacles come your way. The dictionary defines perseverance this way: "To hold to a course, belief, or goal in spite of the obstacles." Life without obstacles is totally unrealistic, so when they do face us, we need to persevere. Perseverance is a life skill which unlocks the abilities God has entrusted to each of us, enabling us to become what he intended us to be. The snails had to persevere to make it to the ark before it sailed. They never gave up and neither should we. The benefits of persevering in righteousness and love are clearly reflected by the verse above: life, prosperity and honor. What's not to like about those results? So keep on keeping on and never give up!

CONTENTMENT: THE ATTITUDE OF GRATITUDE

"I have learned in whatever state I am, to be content." **Common Sense from the Bible—*Phil. 4:11* (NKJV)**

Zig Ziglar liked to say that this verse proves that Paul was not a Texan because no true Texan would ever be content in any other state! Seriously, our contentment should never depend on our comfortable circumstances, material possessions or freedom from pain or sorrow. It must come from our relationship with God and the realization of how much he has given and forgiven. The word that best describes contentment is gratitude, which comes from two words: GReat ATTITUDE! We practice it by being thankful for what we have rather than focusing on what we think we lack. Our tendency is to count the blessings God gives others, which blinds us to his gifts to us. So, count your blessings and be content with what God has done!

These are *PocketPowerPrimers*...copy them often and cut them up to carry with you for regular review to keep your "pump of life primed." You can also share them with others for their encouragement such as leaving one with your tip in restaurants.

HABITS: YOU ARE WHAT THEY ARE
"Although I want to do good, evil is right there with me."
Common Sense from the Bible—Rom. 7:21 (NIV)

The struggle between good and evil Paul refers to above is supported by the lyrics of a song by Bob Dylan: "It may be the devil or it may be the Lord/But you're gonna have to serve somebody." Our lives are governed by which one we choose. And which one we choose determines the habits we develop—right or wrong. We all want to do what is right but the tendency is always there to do wrong. If we don't fight that tendency, it will soon become a bad habit such as being sarcastic, critical, impatient or worse. And it takes enormous effort to change a bad habit. The best way is to replace them with good ones which may require a change in who you're serving. Per Dylan, there are only two choices . . . we either serve the devil or the Lord!

CHOICES: PLANTING YOUR HARVEST
"Don't be misled . . . You will always harvest what you plant."
Common Sense from the Bible —Gal. 6:7

It's all their fault, right? Adam and Eve had it made until Satan—history's first scammer—came along. They chose to believe him rather than obey God, and they ate the forbidden fruit. When God confronted them, they blamed the serpent, and the poor snake didn't have a leg to stand on! Starting with the first family, history is filled with ruined lives due to bad choices. While our poor choices won't affect human history as theirs did, ours can have devastating results in our lives and the lives of loved ones. Choices must be made carefully and prayerfully. A simple question to ask when facing hard choices is: *What does God desire for me*? The good news is that even after a bad choice, it's never too late to change course!

PRIDE AND HUMILITY
"God opposes the proud but favors the humble."
Common Sense from the Bible —James 4:6

"Pride goes before the fall." Everyone has heard that old saying, and it's as true today as ever. Just look at political, entertainment, sports, even religious circles, and you'll see long lists of those whose pride preceded humiliating falls from positions of power, fame and fortune. It's normal to want to be recognized. If it happens, be humbly thankful. You can be sure that God does see everything we do, and he rewards those things done that honor him! So, use the talents and abilities God gave you, do your best to glorify him, and you'll eliminate the risk of falling due to pride. This statement puts all this in the right perspective: We make the most difference when we don't know we're making a difference!

These are *PocketPowerPrimers*...copy them often and cut them up to carry with you for regular review to keep your "pump of life primed." You can also share them with others for their encouragement such as leaving one with your tip in restaurants.

TEMPTATION: A COMMON AFFLICTION

"The temptations in your life are no different from what others experience." Common Sense from the Bible—*1 Cor. 10:13*

Temptations are battles with history's first scammer, the devil Satan. He is a deceiver and devilishly subtle, and if you think you can win an argument with him, you're wrong. He always shows us the bait, usually pleasure, but not the hook, which is always pain. Being tempted is an alarm that warns us of sin's danger. Giving in to temptation is sin. There are two ways to avoid giving in . . . in James 4:7 we read: "Resist the devil and he will flee from you." The even better option is found in 2 Timothy 2:22 where Paul says: "Run from whatever is tempting you." In other words, stop, drop and run. Maybe if we had to pay the price in advance for giving in to them, temptations wouldn't be so difficult to handle!

EMOTIONS ARE NORMAL

"Jesus wept."
Common Sense from the Bible—*John 11:35*

The shortest verse in the Bible refers to the strongest man in history weeping. Jesus wept in sorrow over his friend's death. Tears can come from feelings of joy, love, fear, frustration, anger, loss, sadness, sorrow and other emotions. Emotions are facts of life. They play a huge role in our daily lives because our response to any situation involves emotions. If our emotions are caused by negative situations, we can take our concerns to God for consolation and perspective. Feelings are fickle. You may be feeling down, but if the phone rings, you answer it and act like everything's fine. You might not win an Oscar, but you did just prove that y*ou don't feel your way into a new way of acting—you act your way into a new way of feeling!*

GOD'S SOLUTION TO OUR POLLUTION

"Everyone has sinned; we all fall short of God's glorious standard."
Common Sense from the Bible—*Rom. 3:23*

How long can you go without sinning? We are all polluted with sin. It is a human addiction. Sin always takes us farther than we intended to stray, keeps us longer than we intended to stay, and costs us more than we intended to pay! Can you relate to that? Or maybe to this: "I want to do what is good, but I don't. I don't want to do what is wrong, but I do it anyway." That was written by the apostle Paul in Romans 7:19. He wrote many books of the Bible, so if you can relate to that, you're in pretty good company! What to do? Well, in Micah 7:19, God tells us if we confess our sins, he will "throw them into the depths of the ocean." That's God's solution to our sin pollution. So don't go deep-sea diving to bring back what he has deep-sixed!

These are *PocketPowerPrimers*...copy them often and cut them up to carry with you for regular review to keep your "pump of life primed." You can also share them with others for their encouragement such as leaving one with your tip in restaurants.

FORGIVING OTHERS IS NOT OPTIONAL

"Forgive anyone who offends you . . . the Lord forgave you, so you must forgive others." Common Sense from the Bible—Col. 3:13

We can't comprehend true forgiveness because, as difficult as it is to forgive, we can't forget. Because of that, we don't understand how God can do both, which plants doubts about God's forgiveness of us. However, his grace, available through Jesus' sacrifice on the cross, has the power to forgive even the most serious sin. To prove that, while on that cruel cross, Jesus even offered this prayer, recorded in Luke 23:34, for those who put him there: "Father forgive them, for they don't know what they are doing." He still prays that prayer for us. Until we experience his forgiveness, we can't forgive others. Only then as forgiven people, can we (and we must) forgive others out of gratitude for what Jesus did for us—it's not an option!

THE FEAR FACTOR

"God has not given us a spirit of fear . . . but of power, love, and self-discipline." Common Sense from the Bible—2 Tim. 1:7

Fear is a very real human emotion which we all deal with as did most of the heroes of faith and even Jesus. The most oft-repeated phrase in the Bible is to *"fear not"* or *"do not be afraid."* We often deal with fear because much about life is scary. Jesus' own disciples flipped out when their boat—with Jesus in it—was caught in a storm. Though Jesus is not physically with us, he does know what "boat" we're in during life's storms because his Spirit is there with us. And it's perfectly okay to cry out for his help when we feel like our boat is sinking. In fact, that's exactly what he wants us to do. Thankfully, much of what we fear doesn't come to pass. The letters in the word FEAR remind us of that fact: False Evidence Appearing Real!

FAITH AND FACT FIGHT FEAR AND FEELINGS

In all things God works for the good of those who love him. Common Sense from the Bible—Rom. 8:28 (NIV)

This well-known verse should be a real *faith* builder. However, chaotic situations in the world and in our lives can create *feelings* of doubt about the *fact* of God's presence, power and purpose. In those circumstances, *fear* can nearly overwhelm our *faith*, and the *fact* of God's love seems to lack the evidence we desperately need. But God is in control, and all things do work together for good for all who love him. This may help: *Three were walking in God's will and way: Feelings, Faith and Fact. When Fear came up and tried to stay, Feelings began to sway. Faith then faltered if truth be told, but Fact stayed strong and bold. Fact fought Fear and Faith came back, and Feelings, too, got back on track.* Faith and fact always win the fight!

These are *PocketPowerPrimers*...copy them often and cut them up to carry with you for regular review to keep your "pump of life primed." You can also share them with others for their encouragement such as leaving one with your tip in restaurants.

PRAYER IS POWER
"Don't worry about anything; instead, pray about everything."
Common Sense from the Bible—*Phil. 4:6*

Simple, right? Not so simple to practice! In good times, it's easy not to pray. In tough times it's easier to worry than to pray. If we do pray and don't see an answer when and how we expect, we doubt prayer's power. It may seem like our prayers are bouncing off heaven's ceiling, but they aren't. God answers *all* prayers in one of four ways:

1. When the *request* is not right—God says *no.*
2. When *you* are not right—God says *grow.*
3. When the *time* is not right—God says *slow.*
4. When *everything* is right—God says *go!*

The Bible tells us to pray continually. That probably implies praying with your eyes open—especially if you're driving!

WHY GO TO CHURCH?
"I was glad when they said to me, 'Let us go to the house of the Lord.'" **Common Sense from the Bible—*Ps. 122:1***

Glad to go to church? Let's get real! Going to church is not something we naturally desire to do, is it? After disobeying God by taking bites of the forbidden fruit, Adam and Eve tried to hide from him. And people have been trying to hide from him ever since! But God created us as multidimensional beings and wants fellowship with us. Our spiritual dimension is God-shaped. Admit it or not, missing that part of life is like missing one piece of a puzzle—frustrating and incomplete. There are many excuses for not going to church. One of the most common is that there are a lot of hypocrites there. That may be true, but there's always room for one more! There are many good reasons to go to church. Is there any good reason not to?

CREATION OR EVOLUTION?
"The entire universe was formed at God's command."
Common Sense from the Bible—*Heb. 11:3*

This verse is the Bible's answer to the question about the origin of the universe. There are questions about how creation took place, but there are many more about the theory of evolution. For instance, if the earth is a sphere in the universe, what keeps it in space? Why don't the oceans and lakes spill out? Obviously it's gravity. But gravity doesn't evolve, so how did it get there? Evolution had to start with something,—how did "something" get there? The universe is packed full of undeniable evidence of the Creator in whose image we are created. There's also evidence that our Creator has a wonderful sense of humor. What did Adam think when he first saw an ostrich—a big bird with little wings that can't fly but can outrun a horse?

Ten Reasons Not To Be A Christian

1. *I've done some really bad things that I'm sure God can't forgive.* Wrong—God has promised to forgive and forget all our sins!

2. *I won't be the same person.* Change is always difficult, but we can all benefit from a change for the better!

3. *It would take the fun out of life.* Actually, life is more fun when you're not worrying about dying—way more fun!

4. *I'll lose control of my life.* If you think about it, that might be a good thing—how much of your life do you control anyway?

5. *I'm afraid of what my friends will think.* What God thinks is more important—maybe you should change friends!

6. *I'm too busy to go to church.* We all are. But we all find time for what we feel is important—worshipping God is important!

7. *I don't understand Christianity.* You might not fully understand electricity either—but you probably aren't living in the dark!

8. *Christianity has too many unknowns.* Much about life is unknown but one thing is sure, life is fatal and you will die—then what?

9. *Christianity is boring.* Jesus came to give us an abundant life now and eternal life when we die—boring? Not!

10. *Christians are hypocrites.* Well, aren't we all? But Christians are forgiven—making us recovering hypocrites!

A FINAL THOUGHT . . .
ON GOD'S ETERNAL LIFE INSURANCE

Several times in this book you have read that God offers an eternal life insurance policy that has no fine print, and for which the premium has already been paid. At the risk of being redundant, I want to share some last thoughts on how the premium on that policy was paid.

Jesus paid that premium. But to understand what he went through to pay it, you need to read Luke 22 and 23. It is a horror story of cruel torture, ending with the gruesome murder of Jesus by hanging on a cross until his lifeblood ran out. If you don't want to read all the gory details, I understand. But don't miss verses 39-43 of chapter 23, which detail a dramatic scene that played out just before Jesus died.

You see, on either side of Jesus' cross there were crosses on which two criminals were also being hung. As the crowds loudly jeered and scoffed at Jesus, one of the criminals mocked him by saying, "If you're really the Messiah, save yourself—and us too, while you're at it!" But the other criminal recognized him as the Messiah and said, "Jesus, remember me when you come into your kingdom." Jesus reassured him, saying, "Today you will be with me in paradise."

Immediately, that criminal, regardless of how bad he had been, was renewed as God's masterpiece. If you get the chance before you die, will you ask Jesus to remember you? If you haven't asked him yet, it would be well to do it without delay—it's a matter of heaven or hell. The sooner you ask that question and get it answered, the sooner you can enjoy masterpiece living while you're still alive!